TORNADO ADV

TORNADO ADV
THE LAST COLD WAR INTERCEPTOR

PETER FOSTER

The History Press

Front cover: Silhouetted against a setting sun, Tornado F.3 ZE257 'UB' of No.43 Squadron is seen at a height above 30,000ft during a practice 'QRA' scramble from RAF Leuchars on 13 January 2005.

Rear cover: Clean and arrow-shaped, the Tornado F.3 epitomises the shape of an interceptor. Captured over the Irish Sea off the coast of the Isle of Man on 3 October 2008, ZE764 'GL' in No.43 Squadron markings was once the mount of Wing Commander David Hamilton of No.XI Squadron. Today it forms part of the final chapter of the F.3 story as it sees its days out with No.111 Squadron.

Rear cover: No.111 Squadron patch – it says it all.

Other books by the author:

Sepecat Jaguar: Endangered Species – 978-0-7524-3859-7
Tornado: A History – 978-0-7524-4514-4

First published 2011
The History Press
The Mill, Brimscombe Port,
Stroud, Gloucestershire, GL5 2QG
www.thehistorypress.co.uk

© Peter Foster 2011

British Library Cataloguing in Publication Data.
A catalogue record for this book is available from the British Library.

ISBN 978 0 7524 5936 3

Typesetting, design and origination by The History Press.
Printed in Great Britain

CONTENTS

PREFACE

TORNADO ADV IS designed as a pictorial tribute to an aircraft that has had its fair share of criticism, but one that perhaps started life as an ugly duckling, only to grow into a well-respected swan. Clean and in full wing sweep the Panavia Tornado ADV epitomises what a fast interceptor should look like. It is impressive in looks, and, in the twilight of its career, very capable.

Never conceived as a dogfighter, advances in missile technology and the advent of JTIDS eventually turned the jet into a very respectable war fighter and one that in a scenario of its own choosing could hold its own with the best of them.

In this pictorial history I have attempted to chronicle the life of the ADV, although I cannot claim that every change of marking or special colour scheme is included. However, I hope that most will be found over the following pages.

I am indebted to a number of friends and colleagues who have assisted in supplying information and a few supplementary photographs. Above all I have to thank Danny Bonny, the editor of the much respected *British Aviation Review*, for allowing me to use verbatim several passages from the 1993 and 1996 issues of the magazine.

The text is not intended to be a definitive history but does, I hope, capture most of the main significant events, both operationally and technically, that have shaped the aircraft's career.

Peter R. Foster
Doddington
Cambs

'The Office.'

INTRODUCTION

THE RAF'S REQUIREMENT for a Lightning replacement was drafted as long ago as 1971 under Air Staff Target 395, although the concept of an aircraft to defend UK airspace from Soviet bombers had been drawn up in 1968 when the original requirement for the Tornado IDS version had been conceived. At that time the Multi-Role Combat Aircraft (MRCA) concept had been gathering momentum.

In conceiving Tornado ADV the mission profile demanded an aircraft with powerful radar, high transit speed and a healthy range. The net result was the Tornado F.3 but the design was over-specialised and in today's very budget-conscious environment perhaps a luxury.

Given the benefit of hindsight one wonders whether the Tornado ADV would have ever made the final cut and perhaps other equally good, and possibly cheaper, options might have fulfilled the requirement and given options for other roles. It was clear from the finished result that the aircraft was to meet all the original requirements and, with the advances in avionic and missile technology, far more. However it never was, and never would be, a dogfighter.

The heart of the ADV version of the Tornado was the newly developed GEC-Marconi AI.24 Foxhunter radar – a frequency-modulated interrupted continuous wave (FMICW) set operating in the 3cm I-band. Built by Marconi-Elliot (with Ferranti as a major sub-contractor), the company received the contract to develop the radar back in 1976, building on existing radars which had been flying in experimental and trials aircraft for a number of years.

The radar consisted of eight liquid-cooled LRUs clustered around a central transmitter. The front was predominantly analogue, with a coherent travelling wave tube transmitter giving high power over a range of bandwidths. It incorporated a J-band illuminator for Skyflash or similar semi-active radar homing missiles, whilst the antenna was a light and simple conventional twist-cassegrain variety that gave greater consistency and lower side lobes than the newer planar arrays.

The radar incorporated a sophisticated track-while-scan capability and was extremely user-friendly with its synthetic symbology clearly displayed and easy to manipulate. Original thinking also envisaged the aircraft having an electro-optical Visual Augmentation System (VAS) and the crews having helmet-mounted sights, but this proved a little too optimistic.

The Tornado ADV's teeth were built around the BAE Systems Skyflash missile, a British derivative of the AIM-7E-2 Sparrow which used an externally identical airframe, but with an improved seeker and fuse. It also had a marginally longer range.

The missile had been developed initially in 1969 and ordered in 1973 for use by the RAF's F4K/M Phantoms but the derivative designed for Tornado was a fire-and-forget version incorporating mid-course inertial guidance and an active radar terminal guidance unit.

For short-range engagements the Tornado ADV was equipped with four AIM-9 Sidewinder AAMs although it was expected that these would eventually be supplemented by the AIM-132 ASRAAM: a missile that had been ordered by the RAF but ironically not for Tornado F.3.

Three Tornado ADV prototypes were ordered and these were basically to the same specification as the Tornado F.2 that followed. All three aircraft were fully equipped with a comprehensive air-to-ground telemetry system, which allowed real-time analysis of test-point manoeuvres and clearance for the pilot to proceed to continue testing at more severe conditions of speed, altitude, roll-rage, g-factors and so on.

The first of these jets, ZA254, was rolled at Warton on 9 August 1979 and undertook its maiden flight on 27 October 1979, which lasted 1 hour 32 minutes.

The first production aircraft were delivered to the RAF to an interim standard without automatic wing sweep and the ability to carry only two underwing AIM-9 Sidewinder missiles. The aircraft also lacked a working radar as Foxhunter had been delayed by a multitude of technical problems and, as has become commonplace with the RAF, effectively moving goal posts.

It was not until June 1981 that one of the prototypes, ZA283, was to fly with the new radar and the first twenty production sets were not delivered until July 1983, by which time the radar was four years late and more than 50 per cent over budget. Even then it was not until mid-1985 that Warton began delivering aircraft with radar installed. In the meantime the Tornado F.2s carried on with just ballast in the front end with the exception of the final deliveries.

Eventually it is believed all the Tornado F.2s were received with PP radar fitted allowing a limited degree of realistic role training. The aircraft had sufficient combat capability to allow the unit, 229 OCU, to be declared to NATO as an emergency air defence unit in May 1985.

Seen here on its maiden flight from Warton, Eric Bucklow and Les Hurst get the first production air defence version of the Tornado into the air on 12 April 1984. ZD899, known in company terms as AT001, was, however, not the first of the new breed to fly, with AT002 (ZD900) undertaking its first flight on 5 March. ZD899 was destined to be retained as part of the BAE Systems test and development fleet until retired on 30 June 2004, over twenty years later.

The log book of Eric Bucklow, showing the first flight of ZD899.

Year 1984		AIRCRAFT		Captain or 1st Pilot	Co-pilot 2nd Pilot Pupil or Crew	DUTY (including number of day or night landings as 1st Pilot or Dual)
Month	Date	Type and Mark	No			
—	—	—	— —	—	—	— Totals brought forward
APR	5	CESS 402B	G-BADT	STOCK	SELF	TYPE RATING
	6	TOR GR.1	BS117	SELF	SMITH	P2
	10	"	BS116		"	P3
	12	TOR F.2	AT1		HURST	P1 FMN WITH XL586
	13	CANB TT.18	WK118		MALINGS	RADIO TRIAL. SAMLESBURY - HURN
	16	"	"		" /CHANT	TARGET TOWING
	17	"	"		" / "	"
	17	"	"		" / "	"
	18	"	"		"	HURN - SAMLESBURY

CHAPTER 1

SERVICE ENTRY

THE FIRST TORNADO ADV for the RAF, F.2 variant ZD901, arrived at Coningsby on 5 November 1984 in company with ZD903. Four days previously, the first Tornado ADV unit, which was to become No.229 Operational Conversion Unit, had unofficially formed under the command of then Wing Commander 'Rick' Peacock-Edwards. During the coming months, instructor crews for the OCU underwent training on the new fighter with British Aerospace (BAe), with 229 OCU officially forming at Coningsby on 1 May 1985. The ability to conduct 'in-house' training came ten days later, following the completion of the second instructor course at Warton. It was expected that the OCU would have a full strength of twenty-two aircraft in 1987.

The first Tornado F.2 to be delivered to the RAF was ZD901 when it was delivered to Coningsby on 11 November 1984. It joined 229 OCU under the watchful gaze of Wing Commander Rick Peacock-Edwards as 'AA', although was later recoded 'AB' just prior to being flown to St Athan in October 1987 for storage. It was later to give up its centre fuselage section to ZE154, the first F.3 that had been damaged during overhaul.

Seen taking off from RAF Coningsby in a clean configuration during instructor crew validation is ZD932, sporting 229 OCU markings and coded 'AM'. The jet had been delivered to the unit on 29 April 1985 on its fourth flight and was to see less than two years' service before passing into storage. It too gave up its centre fuselage to repair a damaged F.3, with the forward section then being used by the BDRT flight at St Athan.

The unit took part in its first air defence exercise, Exercise Priory 85/2, between 21–23 October 1985. By this time, sixteen Tornado F.2s were on strength and training of instructors continued into 1986 despite delivery problems with the Foxhunter radar systems for the aircraft. 229 OCU was selected to provide a diamond-nine formation for the Queen's Birthday Flypast on 14 June 1986 involving ZD901, 903, 934, 904, 935, 932, 937, 940 and 941; the first time that a Tornado fighter squadron would mount such an occasion.

Reports in the press at the time cited Foxhunter had been accepted but needed numerous modifications to bring it up to a more acceptable specification. It was alleged at the time that the system needed a larger computer, something that could have been chosen at the start of the project. It was also reported that,

The last production Tornado F.2 ZD941, although being nominally on the strength of 229 OCU, undertook some trials work during its brief year of operational use. It is seen here undertaking Skyflash air-to-air missile firing integration trials. The missile then used by both the RAF Phantom force and the Swedish Air Force JA 37 Viggen aircraft was a semi-active radar homing missile with a monopulse seeker.

It wasn't until the advent of the Tornado F.3 version that the RAF got its hands on an effective air defence system. Delays in delivery and acceptance of the AI.24 Foxhunter radar had effectively seen the earlier F.2 versions as a general handling platform, whereas the F.3 brought with it some teeth. Here ZE162, the eighth production F.3, is seen in a climb equipped with four Skyflash and two AIM-9 Sidewinder missiles. The jet carries the markings of No.65 (Shadow) Squadron. The version of the nose marking was later altered to a chevron.

No.29 Squadron formed in 1987 as the first front-line Tornado F.3 squadron and was followed in December 1987 by No.5 Squadron. Even in those early days there was to be the borrowing of jets as depicted in this photograph. ZE256 'CT' of No.5 Squadron is flanked by No.29 Squadron example ZE206 'BF' and No.65 Squadron example ZE250 'AF' during this OCU-generated sortie in March 1988.

One of the first front-line pilots to convert to the Tornado F.3 was Tony Paxton. A former Lightning pilot with over 1,000 hours on type with Nos 19 and later 5 Squadrons, Tony went on to fly the IDS version of the Tornado with No.31 Squadron and was thus ideally placed to transfer back to the air defence force when the Tornado F.3 was taken into service. He is seen here in ZE209 'BC' of No.29 Squadron leading a three-ship over the North Sea and captured on refuelling area 6 on 14 July 1987.

such a system was considered too high and too risky for a tight budget. Saving money in the short term on Foxhunter's brain subsequently proved to be a false economy. It was not until the software interface between radar and cockpit display was eventually sorted out that the aircraft was to get anywhere near what was required.

The first operational F.3 variant, which incorporated the uprated RB199 Mk104 turbo fans, was ZE159 and this was delivered to RAF Coningsby on 28 July 1986 to join the OCU, coinciding with the unit taking on shadow squadron status as No.65 [Reserve] Squadron. As the months went past, the new F.3s replaced the less capable F.2 variants, the majority of which found their way to No.19 MU at RAF St Athan for storage. Plans to incorporate some of the F.3-updated equipment (the proposed F.2A variant) were eventually abandoned, the aircraft instead undergoing spares recovery and eventual scrapping.

Training for the first front-line personnel began in December 1986, although just prior to this the unit participated in Exercise Swift Sword in Oman with two aircraft, including ZE165, and, on the first day of 1987, 229 OCU itself was declared to SACEUR (NATO Supreme Allied Commander Europe) as combat-ready in an emergency air defence role. This unusual move was made to alleviate the delays incurred by the entire training programme (caused by the radar problems), and permitted the OCU to take on the 'shadow' identity of No.65 [Reserve] Squadron. This remained the case until July 1992 when, following the disbandment of Phantom-equipped 56 Squadron at RAF Wattisham, 229 OCU/65 Squadron was re-designated the Tornado F.3 OCU/No.56 [Reserve] Squadron as part of the RAF's policy to preserve historic squadron number plates (in turn doing away with numbered OCUs).

The Tornado F.3 Operational Evaluation Unit (commonly referred to as the F3OEU) was formed at Coningsby on 1 April 1987 under Wing Commander Malcolm Gleave. The unit, parented by the Central Trials and Tactics Organisation (CTTO) at HQ Strike Command, operated around three to four aircraft at any one time and utilised them to test various systems and procedures before service release for use by front-line squadrons. For example, the unit trialled the Joint Tactical Information and Distribution System (JTIDS) data-link project prior to use by the Coningsby wing. This unit eventually came under the umbrella of the newly formed Air Warfare Centre at

in those early days, due to the system not being fully automatic, the cockpit workload was exceptionally high. Further than that the radar could get deceived too easily in close combat when rapid manoeuvring demands higher brainpower to cope with the situation awareness in a high-energy environment.

It was alleged that when the specification was laid down, those involved had not envisaged the aircraft as being anything other than a long-range bomber destroyer with little or no need to enter the close air threat dogfight environment. Had more investment been available and an automatic system been introduced at the outset then the early years may have been different. As it was,

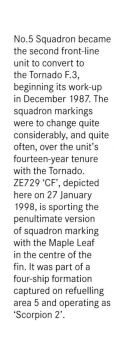

No.5 Squadron became the second front-line unit to convert to the Tornado F.3, beginning its work-up in December 1987. The squadron markings were to change quite considerably, and quite often, over the unit's fourteen-year tenure with the Tornado. ZE729 'CF', depicted here on 27 January 1998, is sporting the penultimate version of squadron marking with the Maple Leaf in the centre of the fin. It was part of a four-ship formation captured on refuelling area 5 and operating as 'Scorpion 2'.

The first of the Leeming-based squadrons to transition to the Tornado F.3 was No.XI. Conversion began in April 1988; the squadron's first Commanding Officer was Wing Commander David Hamilton, another former Lightning and Phantom pilot who was thus well-placed to view the pros and cons of the single-seat/twin-seat discussion. A charismatic character who features in Bob Prest's book *F4 Phantom*, he was to be lead F.3 force Commanding Officer under Operation Desert Shield. Depicted here is aircraft ZE788 'DC', seen at Leeming in February 1989.

No.23 Squadron became the second RAF Leeming squadron to transition to the Tornado F.3. It also became the shortest user of the type, succumbing to defence savings announced in the 1993 White Paper that reduced the Tornado ADV force from 122 to 100 operational airframes. No.23 Squadron utilised the Tornado F.3 for barely six years but was fortunate to receive aircraft with the stage 1 upgrade to the troublesome Foxhunter radar, thus avoiding the 'Z' version that was significantly deficient against the original operational requirement. Aircraft ZE832 'EB', depicted here at Leeming in February 1989, saw only limited RAF service, being transferred to the Italian Air Force in 1995 and scrapped upon its return in 2003.

RAF Waddington and when the SAOEU from Boscombe Down relocated to RAF Coningsby in March 2004 the two units were combined under one command. Then, following the disbandment of No.41 Squadron at RAF Coltishall, the unit took on the reserve title of No.41 [Reserve] Squadron.

No.29 Squadron, having relinquished its Phantom FGR.2s on 31 March 1987, was to be the first front-line unit to operate the Tornado F.3. The squadron became operational on 1 November 1987, having begun its work-up in the previous May, under the command of Wing Commander Lloyd Doble. The unit had the distinction of mounting Operation Golden Eagle between 21 August and 25 October 1988 as part of the 70th anniversary of the RAF's formation, with four aircraft circumnavigating the globe during the sixty-six-day tour of the Far East, Australasia and the USA. In the course of the operation the four jets, ZE254 'BG', ZE288 'BI', ZE728 'BS' and ZE759 'BT', visited Oman and Butterworth in Malaysia for Exercise Lima Bersatu 88, before attending the Australian bicentennial airshow at Richmond. The showpiece deployment was equally as much about a sales drive on behalf of BAE Systems and it brought forth interest from Oman, Malaysia and Saudi Arabia.

The re-equipment of other units followed, with No.5 Squadron moving to RAF Coningsby from RAF Binbrook in December 1987 to begin work-up on the F.3; the unit was declared to SACEUR on 1 May 1988. No.11 Squadron was next, having been the last unit to operate the much-loved Lightning up until May 1988 and, following work-up at Coningsby, became the first squadron to operate from the newly refurbished RAF Leeming from July 1988.

No.11 Squadron, preferring the title XI(F) Squadron, was declared to SACLANT (NATO Supreme Allied Commander Atlantic) in the

The last Leeming squadron to convert to the Tornado F.3 was No.25 Squadron, which did so on 1 April 1989. Again this squadron was to receive the stage 1 Foxhunter radars and its first two jets were ZE838 and ZE858. Squadron markings were, however, not to be the unit's strong point, although in this particular shot depicting ZE737 'FF' and unmarked No.XI Squadron example ZE983 'DN', the squadron's Hawk on the mailed fist is quite prominent. Taken on 14 November 1996 on refuelling area 11, the two aircraft concerned were part of a package of four, using the call-signs 'Javelin 2 & 3' respectively.

maritime air defence role on 1 November 1988. Unlike the other two units that were to join them at the North Yorkshire station, No.11 Squadron operated from a flight-line as opposed to a HAS complex for, in times of tension, the unit would forward-deploy to Stornoway or St Mawgan.

The second of the planned three Leeming squadrons was to be No.23 Squadron (which, having been stationed in the Falkland Islands since 1983, passed its Phantoms to the resurrected 1435 Flight), and the unit began to receive aircraft during the summer of 1988; No.23 Squadron became operational on 1 August 1989 under the command of Wing Commander Neil Taylor.

No.25 Squadron was finally chosen as the third Leeming unit during the spring of 1989, the squadron having previously operated the Bloodhound II missile until 30 September 1989 (its last fixed-wing assignment was on Javelin FAW.7s and FAW.9s

until disbanding on 31 December 1962); Wing Commander 'Flick' Martin's new unit was declared combat-ready with the Tornado on 1 January 1990.

RAF Leuchars was to be the last station to receive the F.3, with No.43 Squadron taking delivery of its first two aircraft during Leuchars' 'Battle of Britain at Home Day' on 29 September 1989. No.43 Squadron was declared to SACLANT on 1 July 1990 under the leadership of Wing Commander Andy Moir, the squadron being tasked to maritime air defence in addition to No.11 Squadron.

The final Tornado F.3 squadron to form was No.111 Squadron, which accepted its first aircraft during the early spring of 1990, although the unit's markings were not adorned on an airframe until June of that year. Wing Commander Peter Walker declared the unit operational on 31 December 1990. BAe had delivered

No.43 (F) Squadron F.3 ZE341 'GO' in totally clean configuration low level in LFA 7. The jet has just a single dummy training round ASRAAM on the port station and is in full wing sweep. This shot was taken just prior to the unit inactivating, although the aircraft is now with 111 Squadron and is likely to be one of the last Tornado F.3s in service.

the 800th Tornado on 9 January 1990 and this was the 150th production F.3.

August 1990 saw the start of great upheavals in the fleet due to RAF commitments in the Gulf region under Operation Granby. Following the Iraqi invasion of Kuwait on 2 August 1990, HM Government dispatched a squadron of Tornado F.3s to Dhahran, Saudi Arabia, as part of the growing international military force to deter further Iraqi aggression. No.29 Squadron were just coming to the end of their annual Armament Practice Camp (APC) at Akrotiri, Cyprus, when the invasion took place and No.5 Squadron had just arrived on the island to commence their APC detachment. Six aircraft from each unit, together with a mix of air and ground crews, deployed to Dhahran on 11 August as No.5 [Composite] Squadron (as OC 5

Squadron, Wing Commander Euan Black, led the contingent), with the first combat air patrol (CAP) being flown the next day.

Back in the UK, plans were being formulated for the deployment of Tornado F.3s that carried the latest equipment to replace those already in theatre. These modifications, known as Stage 1+, incorporated: the GEC-Marconi Foxhunter improved Type AA radar; hands on throttle and stick (HOTAS) controls; GEC-Marconi Hermes RHWRs; twin Tracor ALE-40(V) flare dispensers; an improvement to the RB.199 Mk104 throttle controls that could deliver an extra 5 per cent combat power; 'Have Quick' jam-resistant UHF radios; radar absorbent material (RAM) on the leading edges of the fin and wings; and also the ability to carry the Skyflash 90 and AIM-9M variant of the Sidewinder missile.

Pulling high over Cader Idris to avoid a conflicting Hawk movement, ZE207 'GC' has been a long-time member of No.43 (F) Squadron. First noted as 'GC' in June 1991, apart from a short period with No.56 [R] Squadron in 2003, it remained on squadron strength until 2005 when it was flown to Leeming for RTP.

The first six upgraded aircraft (ZE206/DC, ZE210/DD, ZE936/DF, ZE961/DH, ZE962/DI and ZE968/DJ; with ZE203/DA and ZE934/DV acting as airspares) flew out to Dhahran via Akrotiri on 29 August 1990 to replace the No.29 Squadron examples in theatre. The aircraft were coded in the No.11 Squadron range and the unit, led by Wing Commander David Hamilton, became No.11 [Composite] Squadron. A further six F.3s deployed to Saudi Arabia on 16 September 1990 (consisting of ZE204/DB, ZE942/DG, ZE969/DL, ZE162/DM, ZE982/DP, ZE888/DT; airspares for this deployment being ZE165/DU and ZE963/DX), in turn relieving the No.5 Squadron aircraft.

After a decision was made to increase No.11 [C] Squadron's strength to a 'wartime' eighteen aircraft, the final deployment of six aircraft left RAF Leeming on 22 September 1990, being made-up of F.3s ZE203/DA, ZE907/DK, ZE159/DO, ZE165/DU, ZE941/DW and ZE963/DX (airspares being ZE964/DS and ZE965/DY). Further deployments were made in smaller numbers as aircraft were rotated back to the UK for maintenance.

The Dhahran detachment was re-titled No.43 [C] Squadron on 1 December 1990 under the command of Wing Commander Andy Moir, and remained as such until the unit flew its last operational sortie on 8 March 1991, with all F.3s departing Dhahran by 15 March 1991. During the period of the actual conflict (17 January–28 February 1991), 360 CAPs were flown although, much to the frustration of all involved, the F.3s never achieved any 'kills'.

Cockpit workload can be quite high, especially when the AI.24 Foxhunter radar in the early days failed to achieve its design target-detection range of 100 nautical miles against small fighter-sized targets. It was only after Marconi-funded development of a dual-mode dogfight version, to overcome the inherent disadvantages of the high pulse-repetition frequency required to perform the primary role of long-range bomber detection, that real improvements began being achieved.

Back home to mark the events of Operation Granby, twelve Tornado F.3s participated in the flypast on 21 June 1991, drawn from ZE836/CH, ZE934/DX, ZE983/EZ, ZE199/FL, ZE257/BD, ZE729/BF, ZE758/BH, ZG733/BK, ZE965/V, ZE258/GA, ZE755/GB, ZE207/GC, ZE757/GF and unmarked ZE832.

Wing Commander Andy Moir, with No.43 (F) Squadron, undertook a return goodwill visit to Kuwait to mark the first anniversary celebrations of the country's liberation from Iraq. The squadron flew four jets, ZG755/GM, ZE730, ZE732 and ZE757/GF, from Akrotiri where it had been undertaking its annual armament practice camp (APC). The squadron was to return a few months later for Exercise Free Sky 92 which was also centred on Kuwait.

Just prior to this, Panavia Tornado F.3s were assigned to cover the 1435 Flight tasking in the South Atlantic taking over from the Phantom FGR.2s. The first deployment, which was to remain for some seventeen years under Tornado F.3 dominance, saw four jets deploy from RAF Coningsby via Ascension Island on 6 July 1992. The aircraft involved were ZE209, ZE790, ZE758 and ZE812 with ZE342 and ZE792 acting as airspares for the two elements.

Up at Warton, new production aircraft being delivered from ZG751 onwards were fitted with JTIDS, or Link 16 as it was often known, and the aircraft were being concentrated on RAF Coningsby until the system was fully up and running and declared operational. Certainly the crews felt that at last this gave the Tornado F.3 the edge in battle in having better situation awareness and the ability to choose when to fight and when to disengage.

The aircraft's main computer was reportedly given an additional new processor by 1995 allowing the introduction of new clearer displays (new symbology and new presentation, not new screens). Also, most vitally, a new single board main computer gave improved speed and power, giving full functionality during simultaneous use of Stage Two radar and JTIDS. The planned introduction of a new processor brought all surviving RAF Tornado F.3 radars to Stage Two (AB) standard, allowing automatic target acquisition and tracking, and discrimination of head-on targets through analysis of first and second-stage compressor discs. Meanwhile production continued and the 360th and final production Tornado for the Royal Air Force was handed over on 24 March 1993, when F.3 ZH559 was delivered to No.56 [R] Squadron at RAF Coningsby.

Tornado F.3s continued to deploy around the world in addition to their UK air defence duties. Biannual detachments to Malaysia for ADEX/IADS exercises, as well as participation in 'Red Flag' and 'Distant Frontier' exercises in the US, became regular engagements on squadron calendars. The deployment of eight aircraft to Gioia del Colle, Italy, to provide air cover for UN operations in Bosnia typifies the F.3's 'fire brigade' role on the international stage.

The first such deployment was led by No.11 Squadron and become No.11 (Composite) Squadron. Six aircraft were detached on 19 April 1993 as part of the UNPROFOR response to the deepening crisis in the former Yugoslavia. This increased to eight aircraft in May.

Upgrade of the fleet continued and in October 1993 the decision was taken to fit the fleet with Celcius Tech's BOL chaff dispenser, together with a Vinten flare dispensing system as part of the defensive aids suite upgrade.

Working under 5 ATAF control the Tornado F.3s became part of what is overall known as Operation Deny Flight although varying actions gained UK code-names of Operation Grapple, Operation Endeavour and eventually Operation Decisive Edge. By the

Such has been the problem of identifying users of individual airframes. Here we have ZH555 'PT' in 111 Squadron markings alongside No.43 (F) Squadron's 90th anniversary jet, ZG757, in refuelling area 6 on 30 April 2007. Both were being operated by No.43 (F) Squadron on that day. 'Triple-Nickel' was one of the last Tornado F.3s to be delivered to the RAF and had been laid down as part of an order for Oman that was subsequently cancelled.

beginning of May 1993, Allied fighters had flown 706 operational sorties in response to the UN mandate. No.111 Squadron flew the 5000th Operation Grapple sortie on 23 July 1994 and the deployment ceased at the end of February 1996.

The 1993 Defence White Paper saw a requirement for a £1 billion saving in defence spending, which equated to the loss of one Tornado F.3 squadron. No.23 Squadron was to disband on 31 March 1994 as part of these defence spending cuts; at the same time reducing the Tornado F.3 fleet from 122 to 100 aircraft. As the majority of the squadron's aircraft carried the Stage 1+ upgrade they were re-distributed to other units, permitting less-capable aircraft to be placed in storage or be available for the

planned lease of twenty-four Tornado F.3s to Italy. This draw-down in numbers of the operational fleet, coupled with the loss (in the short-term at least) of a number of airframes that were allegedly damaged whilst undergoing maintenance by civilian contractors, did raise doubts about the availability of resources to participate in any future overseas operations by the RAF, such as the Gulf crisis.

Having said that, since the end of the Cold War Soviet intruder flights had become rare. Between 6 September 1991 and January 1994 not a single Soviet aircraft had approached UK airspace. As a consequence only RAF Leuchars was now mounting the Quick Reaction Alert (QRA) status, although it was manned by rotating squadrons rather than just the local Nos 43 and 111 Squadrons.

During necessary airframe modifications (25FI mods) at RAF St Athan, to where the work had been contracted out, industry damage was found on a number of Tornado F.3 fuselage sections allegedly caused by the contractor. The initial batch of fifteen aircraft had the work undertaken by BAe but it was the second batch of eighteen contracted to Airwork, whose £7 million bid was £4 million lower than BAe's, where the problem lay.

The first four aircraft, ZE292, ZE295, ZE343 and ZE728, had been returned to service following modification when pilots reported handling peculiarities. RAF engineers inspected the airframes and discovered longeron distortion.

The longerons had reportedly been distorted when inappropriate tools were used to remove the light alloy collars which covered fasteners connecting panel to the longerons. The remaining fourteen aircraft undergoing modification by Airwork at St Athan were inspected and twelve were found to be severely damaged, with two more having suffered lighter damage. The contract was cancelled immediately and the work on the aircraft halted whilst options were explored. In the meantime the four completed aircraft were returned to St Athan.

At one stage it was thought that the jets would have to be returned to Panavia for centre fuselage rebuild, but this was a very expensive option and serious consideration was given to scrapping the aircraft prematurely. However it was eventually decided to rebuild the aircraft using the centre fuselage sections from the stored Tornado F.2 fighters, as it had already been decided to scrap these aircraft and not proceed with the F.2A conversion programme.

This was a most cost-effective solution made possible by some incisive thinking on the part of the RAF and industry. BAe was awarded the contract to undertake a trial rebuild of ZE154 using the centre section from ZD901. Both aircraft were removed from storage and trucked to Warton on 24 October 1994. The rebuild was successful and all the sixteen worst damaged aircraft were dealt with in the same way (the two aircraft with more minor damage were simply repaired):

ZE154 received centre fuselage from ZD901
ZE294 received centre fuselage from ZD906
ZE254 received centre fuselage from ZD941
ZE255 received centre fuselage from ZD932
ZE288 received centre fuselage from ZD940
ZE295 received centre fuselage from ZD938
ZE786 received centre fuselage from ZD934
ZE736 received centre fuselage from ZD937
ZE729 received centre fuselage from ZD933
ZE759 received centre fuselage from ZD904
ZE251 received centre fuselage from ZD936
ZE292 received centre fuselage from ZD939
ZE793 received centre fuselage from ZD935
ZE343 received centre fuselage from ZD900
ZE258 received centre fuselage from ZD905
ZE728 received centre fuselage from ZD903

Ironically plans were then put into operation to repair the damaged F.3 centre fuselage sections at DASA for re-use within the Tornado F.3 fleet in a fuselage replacement programme.

The next major event to hit the RAF Tornado F.3 force came during the 1998 Strategic Defence Review (SDR). The Rt Hon. George Robertson MP announced to the House of Commons on 8 July 1998 the removal of a further thirteen Tornado F.3 fighters from the RAF inventory, resulting in the disbandment of a further squadron. In consequence No.29 Squadron at RAF Coningsby disbanded on 31 October 1998. Almost simultaneously, No.43 (F) Squadron became the first RAF squadron to be declared operational with Advanced Medium-Range Air-to-Air Missiles (AMRAAM) and JTIDS.

The next Tornado F.3 squadron to come under the axe of MOD spending cuts was No.5 Squadron at RAF Coningsby. The announcement was made on 1 February 2002 that the squadron would disband by 1 January 2003 and that No.56 [R] Squadron would relocate to RAF Leuchars during April 2003.

No.5 Squadron undertook a farewell flypast of the station on 26 September 2002, disbanding the following day and No.56 [R] Squadron departed for RAF Leuchars on 27 March 2003. All this came at a time when the RAF Tornado F.3 force was still supporting overseas operations both in the Gulf and over Kosovo as part of Operations Resinate and Bolton.

Under the £140 million Tornado F.3 Capability Sustainment Programme (CSP), 100 F.3s were upgraded to incorporate the Raytheon AIM-120 AMRAAM and the Matra BAe Dynamics Advanced Short-Range Air-to-Air Missile (ASRAAM).

Unlike the major detachment during the first Gulf War in 1990–91, the short, sharp action taken in 2003 to topple Saddam Hussein saw very little in the way of air superiority threat and as such the Tornado F.3 force were only to deploy a limited number of aircraft.

Operation Telic, as the UK operation in the second Gulf conflict became known, involved a sizeable number of assets. As far as the Tornado F.3s were concerned, six aircraft were deployed to Al Kharj, Saudi Arabia in January 2003. There were a number of swap overs but the package remained the same. Their involvement in the operation came to an end during the April when the aircraft returned to RAF Leuchars.

RAF Coningsby, now devoid of all of its Tornado F.3 squadrons, was upgraded for the introduction of the Eurofighter Typhoon. Southern 'Q', now re-introduced, was however to remain at the Lincolnshire base with Leeming aircraft and crews deploying to cover the commitment until such time as the Typhoon was considered combat-ready.

During late 2004 consideration was given to enhancing the Tornado F.3's role by equipping the aircraft with ALARM missiles to allow it to undertake a SEAD role. No.XI (F) Squadron undertook the trials and the first aircraft to be noted so fitted was ZE763/DG. The trial, although successful, was ultimately to come to nothing and the SEAD role remained the preserve of the Tornado GR.4.

Geoff Hoon, the then Defence Secretary, announced in Parliament on 21 July 2004 in his 'Delivering Security in a Changing World' speech that there would be further cuts in the Tornado F.3 fleet. He went on to confirm that No.XI (F) Squadron would disband by 31 October 2005 and that Tornado F.3 operation from RAF Leeming would cease by the end of 2008.

At the same moment the RAF was preparing to undertake its first sortie as part of the NATO QRA detachment to Siauliai, Lithuania. Code-named Operation Solstice, four Tornado F.3 aircraft were deployed to protect the Baltic area. The deployment was to last four months with the aircraft returning during January 2005.

No.XI (F) Squadron disbanded on 31 October 2005 followed by No.25 Squadron on 4 April 2008, leaving RAF Leuchars as the sole remaining Tornado F.3 base, although No.56 [R] Squadron also disbanded on 22 April 2008, passing its operational conversion role onto No.43 (F) Squadron.

With the rundown of the Tornado F.3 more or less complete it has only been the delay in Typhoon deliveries, caused to some degree by aircraft being diverted to Saudi Arabia, which has seen the aircraft soldier on until March 2011.

No.43 (F) Squadron disbanded on 13 July 2009, leaving just No.111 Squadron to keep the flag flying for a further eighteen months, bringing an end the story of the RAF's ugly duckling fighter.

Flown by Flight Lieutenant Alex Taylor, this fully armed 'R' jet is seen off the Northumberland coast en route to RAF Leeming, where the Leuchars wing had bolt-holed during runway work at their home station.

CHAPTER 2

RAF CONINGSBY

IN 1966 CONINGSBY was selected as the first base for the RAF fighter-bomber version of the Phantom and it transferred from Bomber Command to Fighter Command. Another period of tremendous building activity, costing some £4.5 million, commenced. In December 1967, because of the initial roles the Phantom was to perform, the station was transferred from Fighter Command to Air Support Command. At the same time, the first ground training course for airmen on the Phantom's systems was started at the No.5 School of Technical training which, in August 1968, became No.3 Squadron of No.228 Operational Conversion Unit. In August 1968 the Phantom FGR 2 arrived at Coningsby, and in October the first aircrew course on the OCU was started in preparation for the formation at Coningsby of the first Phantom squadrons. In October 1974 the station transferred from No.38 Group to No.11 Group, within the now-renamed Strike Command, as its primary role changed from ground attack to air defence.

In March 1976 the Battle of Britain Memorial Flight, which maintains and flies the last of the Royal Air Force's Spitfires and Hurricanes, a Lancaster Bomber and a Dakota, moved to RAF Coningsby from RAF Coltishall.

In 1977 Her Royal Highness, the late Princess Margaret, became Honorary Air Commodore of Royal Air Force Coningsby and visited the station on a biannual basis, until her death on 15 February 2002.

In June 1981 the airfield hardening programme, designed to offer greater protection to aircraft and personnel, began and was finally completed in October 1984. The runway was resurfaced from 1 March until 31 October 1984, during which period operations were carried out from RAF Waddington.

The arrival of the first Tornado F.2 aircraft in November 1984 heralded the next phase in Coningsby's long and varied history. No.229 Operational Conversion Unit was re-formed on 1 November 1984 and quickly began providing crews for the front-line squadrons. The unit was renamed and took on the shadow title of No.65 [Reserve] Squadron but became No.56 [Reserve] Squadron in July 1992. During May 1987, No.29 (F) Squadron gradually phased out its Phantoms and became the first squadron to re-equip with the Tornado F.3, being declared to NATO on 1 November.

No.5 Squadron became the second RAF Coningsby squadron to equip with the Panavia Tornado F.3. Work-up commenced in December 1987 and was declared operational on 1 May 1988.

Prior to this the station became home to the Tornado F.3 Operational Evaluation Unit (F3OEU). The unit was formed as an off-shoot of the Central Trials and Tactics Organisation (CTTO) at Boscombe Down and became the lead element for all system, weapon and tactics changes to effect to Tornado F.3 fleet.

RAF Coningsby remained at the forefront of RAF front-line thinking and in due time were to relinquish the Tornado for the more futuristic Eurofighter Typhoon. The last Tornado F.3 to leave RAF Coningsby did so on 19 December 1987 when the last aircraft assigned to No.41 [Reserve] Squadron, the numberplate assigned to the combined F3OEU/SAOEU (FJ&WOEU), was transferred to the Leuchars wing.

CHAPTER 3
ADV OPERATIONAL CONVERSION

NUMBER 229 OPERATIONAL Conversion Unit (229 OCU), the former Hawker Hunter OCU at RAF Chivenor, was re-formed at RAF Coningsby in 1984 to oversee the introduction and training of the air defence version of the Tornado. Under the watchful gaze of Wing Commander Rick Peacock-Edwards the unit was to receive a compliment of sixteen Tornado F.2 aircraft between November 1984 and November 1985.

Initially committed to instructor training, it was declared to NATO as an emergency air defence unit, as No.65 [R] Squadron, in December 1986, by which time the first Tornado F.3 had arrived. It was at this point the impetus changed to the training of operational crews allowing the conversion of the Phantom and Lightning forces, with Nos 5 and 29 Squadrons the first to transition.

On 1 January 1987 the OCU took on a reserve status as No.65 Squadron, this coinciding with sufficient operationally capable aircraft. At this time No.29 Squadron were still undergoing ground school and as such the 'squadron' was manned by instructors.

No.65 Squadron itself was formed at Wyton on 1 August 1916 from a nucleus flight supplied by Norwich Training Station and

No.65 (Shadow) Squadron was declared to NATO in December 1986 as a limited air defence squadron. At that time it had adopted rectangular nose-bars as depicted in this shot of ZE 167 'AL' seen landing at RAF Coningsby. The jet went on to be part of the second AMI loan package in 1997 and upon return to the UK in March 2004 was earmarked for spares recovery.

229 OCU/No.65 (Shadow) Squadron became No.56 [Reserve] Squadron on 1 July 1992, thus preserving one of the RAF's most famous squadrons. Markings initially consisted of the 'phoenix rising from the flames' emblem on a central position on the fin and rectangular red and white checked nose-bars with the individual aircraft code letters in white, as depicted here on ZE836. This particular aircraft had been one of the original jets delivered to No.23 Squadron in November 1988 and was later to become part of the loan package to the Italian Air Force. It is now preserved as part of the AMI National Collection at Vigna di Valle on the outskirts of Rome.

used a variety of types for training until it left for France with Camels in October 1917. It began flying defensive patrols over the Western Front and in February 1918 began ground attack missions with light bombs on enemy troops and battlefield positions. In August 1918 it moved to the Belgian coastal sector and provided escorts for day bombers attacking enemy bases. During the first weeks of the war it covered the Allied advance into Belgium and returned to the UK in February 1919, disbanding on 25 October 1919.

On 1 August 1934, No.65 re-formed at Hornchurch with Hawker Demons but in September 1935 it began losing its personnel to drafts being sent to the Middle East during the Abyssinian crisis and was reduced to a cadre, being brought up to strength from July 1936, at the same time as Gloster Gauntlets were received to replace the remaining Demons. In June 1937, it re-equipped with Gloster Gladiators, converting to Spitfires in March 1939. In June 1940, offensive patrols began to be flown over France and the Low Countries to cover the evacuation from Dunkirk, the squadron being moved to Lincolnshire to refit at the end of May. It returned south a week later and took part in the Battle of Britain until the end of August, when it moved to Scotland. In November 1940 the squadron moved south again and began

offensive sweeps over northern France in January 1941 before moving to Lincolnshire in February 1941. In October 1941, No.65 received Spitfire Vs which it used for low-level attacks on enemy transport and shipping reconnaissance until October 1942, when it moved back to Scotland. No.65 moved down to Cornwall in March 1943 for fighter patrols and bomber escort missions. In December the squadron converted to North American Mustangs which were used in the fighter-bomber role and in June 1944 No.65 had moved to Normandy where it supported the army until September 1944. The squadron was then moved to East Anglia to act as fighter escorts for Bomber Command's daylight raids over Germany until January 1945 when it moved back to Scotland to provide similar services to Coastal Command attacking shipping off Norway and Denmark.

In May 1945, the squadron moved to East Anglia again where it replaced its Mustangs with Spitfires until June 1946 when it began to receive de Havilland Hornets, moving during the following months to Yorkshire. In December 1950 the squadron began to replace its Hornets with Gloster Meteors and in August 1951 it moved to Duxford. In December 1956, Hawker Hunters began to arrive until No.65 disbanded on 31 March 1961. On 1 January 1964, No.65 re-formed as an anti-aircraft missile unit at Seletar, disbanding on 30 March 1970.

During its tenure at RAF Coningsby 229 OCU/No.65 [Reserve] Squadron did its fair share in promoting the Royal Air Force world wide. Two aircraft, including ZE165/AZ, deployed to Masirah, Oman to participate in Exercise Swift Sword in November 1986. This was in some degree an effort on the part of HMG and BAE Systems to sell the ADV to RAFO and a £500 million order for eight aircraft was forthcoming by January 1988, although this was later cancelled and the airframes were completed for use by the RAF.

The squadron continued to grow in strength beyond the original conceived establishment of twenty-six aircraft with additional Stage 1+ aeroplanes being taken on strength to cover additional Stage 1+ crew training, necessitated by the growing 'out of theatre' commitments. These additional temporary aircraft could be identified by the alpha-numeric codes.

With the continued reduction in RAF strength and the desire to maintain senior and historically important squadrons, No.65 [R] Squadron stood down on 1 July 1992 in favour of No.56

A change of markings for No.65 (Shadow) Squadron occurred quite soon after 229 OCU was re-titled when the nose-bars were altered to a chevron design as depicted here on ZE293 'AC'.

Unit markings and insignia often change either through directive or individual Commanding Officer's choice. By 1995 some of No.56 [Reserve] Squadron's aircraft had begun receiving red and white chequered fin bands and repositioning the code to the rear of the fin. ZE732 'AS', seen here at Fairford, was one of the first although it was to be lost some 30 nautical miles north-east of Flamborough Head on 15 June 1998 whilst being operated by a crew from No.29 Squadron.

Squadron the day after the latter had disbanded as a Phantom FGR.2-equipped front-line air defence unit at RAF Wattisham.

One of the most famous fighter squadrons of the Royal Flying Corps, No.56 Squadron was never a 'shadow' designation in the way that No.65 Squadron had been and as such the No.229 OCU identity was lost entirely.

Number 56 Squadron was originally formed at Fort Rowner, Gosport on 9 June 1916 and soon after set about introducing the new Sopwith SE5 fighter/scout into service. In April 1917, the unit moved to France. Several famous Royal Flying Corps pilots served with the squadron: Captain Albert Ball was a founder member, but was killed in May 1917 and posthumously awarded the VC; Lieutenant A.P.F. Rhys Davids spent a number of months with the squadron and perhaps the most famous Royal Flying Corps pilot of the First World War, Captain James McCudden, arrived with seven victories to his name. Six months later he left with a score

Equally it was often to the non-deployable conversion units that the task of display flying fell. No.56 [Reserve] Squadron, and before that No.65 (Shadow) Squadron, for many years contributed a crew to this task that, along with the Red Arrows, spearheaded the RAF's public relations and recruitment drive. In 1990 aircraft ZE907 received this somewhat outstanding scheme that also marked the 50th anniversary of the Battle of Britain. However, as the aircraft was fitted with the stage 1 radar, when the call to arms came a few months later it hastily had the scheme removed and after receiving the stage 1+ modifications was deployed to the Middle East. The aircraft incidentally served with all RAF Tornado F.3 squadrons with the exception of No.29.

of fifty-seven! By the time the war ended, the squadron claimed 427 victories – all with SE5As.

The post-war cutbacks saw the squadron disband in January 1920, but eight days later it was re-formed at Aboukir, Egypt, this time equipped with Sopwith Snipes. The unit was officially disbanded on 23 September 1922, but elements were hastily formed in a flight and moved to Turkey during the Chanak crisis, remaining in-theatre until August 1923 under the control of

No.208 Squadron at Constantinople. Somewhat confusingly, No.56 Squadron had re-formed at Hawkinge in November 1922!

Between the world wars, the squadron proper flew a succession of biplane fighters until, in May 1938, the Hawker Hurricane arrived. It was with this aircraft that the squadron provided air cover for the Dunkirk evacuation and flew for the entire period of the Battle of Britain in the south of England before replacing them with Hawker Typhoon ground-attack aircraft in September

1941. The full potential of the aircraft was not realised until fighter-bomber operations started in November 1943. Summer 1944 saw the squadron convert to Hawker Tempests and the unit concentrated on anti-V1 ('flying bomb') patrols before moving to France in September. No.56 remained in Germany until it was renumbered No.16 Squadron in March 1946, re-forming the next day at Bentwaters with the renumbering of No.124 Squadron.

The following eight years were spent flying a variety of Gloster Meteor jet fighters until in 1954 the ill-fated Supermarine Swift replaced them. Hawker Hunters arrived in May 1955, and these served until 1961 when the first EE Lightning twin-engined interceptors began to arrive. During the mid-1960s the squadron was chosen as Fighter Command's official demonstration team, and nine aircraft were often seen around the country performing at airshows and deafening the crowd! Following a four-year stay in Cyprus, the squadron converted to Phantoms in 1976, finally retiring the last of these in 1992 when the squadron number was assigned as the Reserve Squadron identity for the Tornado F.3 Operational Conversion Unit at RAF Coningsby. At the end of March 2003, No.56 moved to RAF Leuchars in Fife to allow the airfield to be readied for Eurofighter Typhoon operations.

UNIT MARKINGS

229 OCU: prior to adopting the shadow designation of No.65 [Reserve] Squadron, this unit's markings consisted of a flaming torch crossed by a sword on the centre of the fin (which was retained as mentioned earlier), with codes in black (again in the sequence 'Ax') atop the fin. The nose roundel was placed upon an arrowhead, which was split horizontally with the lower half being red and the top half gold.

No.65 [R] Squadron: this 'shadow' unit became the wartime identity of 229 OCU in January 1987 with its insignia, termed 'in front of fifteen swords in pile, the hilts in base, a lion passant' on a white disc, being applied to the noses of the unit's aircraft. On either side of the marking was originally a white rectangle with opposite direction red chevrons, but that was soon revised to an arrowhead with uni-directional red chevrons, the fuselage roundel being displaced to the air intakes. Codes were in black, in the 'Ax'

sequence, and were placed on the fin above the OCU's flaming torch crossed by a sword motif. Some aircraft received the 229 OCU arrowhead above.

No.56 Squadron: following the re-designation of 229 OCU on 1 July 1992, the 'Firebirds' phoenix emblem began to be applied to the centre-fin of the unit's F.3s. Codes, still in the 'Ax' range of 229 OCU/65[R] Squadron, were applied in white atop the fin (from early 1993 these also began to be edged in red). The nose roundel is flanked by red and white chequered nose-bars.

By July 1995 a number of aircraft began receiving a red/white chequered fin tip band as well and the code was reduced in size and repositioned to the trailing edge of the fin tip. Later the fin tip band was enlarged and the code in white repositioned immediately beneath. At that time the nose marks were also removed.

When No.56 [Reserve] Squadron took over the mantle it produced an even more lavish scheme for the 1993 display season on ZE839 'AR'. Another former No.23 Squadron mount, the jet was to become the first Tornado F.3 to undergo fuselage replacement, undertaking its first flight following overhaul on 31 August 2001.

CHAPTER 4

OPERATIONAL EVALUATION

AIRCRAFT TRIALS AND tactics were once the province of the A&AEE at Boscombe Down but in April 1987 the F.3 Operational Evaluation Unit (F3OEU) was formed at RAF Coningsby as an offshoot of the Central Trials and Tactics Organisation (CTTO) at Boscombe Down. Unlike the plans to form an IDS OEU at a front-line base, mindset had changed and it was felt that the basing of the unit at what was effectively the home of the Tornado F.3 force commander would reap greater benefits.

The F3OEU formed prior to the standing up of the first front-line air defence Tornado F.3 unit and was well placed to undertake the role of developing doctrine and tactics for the ADV force while also conducting trials to evaluate new equipment and systems.

ZH552 was the first of the cancelled Omani order that was delivered to the RAF. At the time the RAF felt it did not need or want these aircraft, but the decision was effectively forced upon them. Originally assigned to No.56 [Reserve] Squadron as 'AZ', it had been transferred to the F3OEU by early 1993. A year later when the Air Warfare Centre came into being it adopted the markings in the picture below and was to retain these for nearly two years until a standardised OEU marking was introduced. The jet is seen here at RAF Waddington on 24 October 1994.

The revision of markings for the F3OEU as part of the overall AWC structure came in 1996. Here we have a shot of ZE982 sporting the changed markings whilst in formation with ZG731 from No.29 Squadron and ZG793 from No.5 Squadron. The jets were all being flown by F3OEU crews and were en route from Bangor, Maine, USA to Lajes on a 'Cyclone Trail'. They had been undertaking a number of trials in the USA including working with US Navy Grumman E-2C Hawkeye AEW aircraft. For this trial utilising JTIDS they operated from Oceana NAS in Virginia.

The concept worked so successfully that with the introduction of the Eurofighter Typhoon, the Tornado F.3's successor, the system has been continued.

In order to keep abreast of developments, the unit continually exchanged its mounts so as to have airframes of the highest modification status whilst also on occasion 'borrowing' aircraft from front-line squadrons.

The RAF were to later create a new Air Warfare Centre (AWC) at nearby RAF Waddington on 1 July 1993, an organisation that incorporated the old CTTO. The AWC was to be responsible for not only the F3OEU but also its strike cousins and, in time, other more sophisticated platforms. As such the organisation adopted a common marking for its assigned aircraft, only differentiating between types by the colour of the chevron. In the case of the F3OEU the chevron was red.

When the Strike Attack Operational Evaluation Unit (SAOEU) transferred to RAF Coningsby from Boscombe Down in April 2004 it was to merge with the F3OEU, and the Air Guided Weapons OEU

Unusually the F3OEU also gained permission to give one of their jets a colourful tail. ZE785 received a crimson tail with the OEU marking centrally displayed and the inscription '1987–2004' to mark the end of the F3OEU prior to its absorption into the FJ&WOEU in March 2004. The jet itself however was no stranger to lavish schemes, having sported a No.65 (Shadow) Squadron 75th Anniversary scheme in 1990 and later No.111 Squadron 90th anniversary scheme in 2008. It is seen here, in this Brian Hodgeson shot, taxiing at RAF Waddington.

(AGWOEU) from RAF Valley, under the auspices of the Fast Jet Weapon Operational Evaluation Unit (FJWOEU).

As well as the development of operational tactics, the role of the FJWOEU is the evaluation of avionics and weapons such as ASRAAM, Brimstone and Storm Shadow, MBDA's precision attack stand-off missile that successfully saw operational service in Operation Telic. The unit's tasks are carried out in close liaison with Defence manufacturers, research institutions and front-line squadrons. The unit took on the mantle of No.41 [R] Squadron in April 2006, following the unit disbanding on the Sepecat Jaguar, and was to operate a mix of air defence and strike attack aircraft until development of the F.3 was completed at the end of 2007. The unit's last Tornado F.3 departed on 19 December on transfer to RAF Leuchars.

On 1 April 2010 No.41 [R] Squadron took on the title of Test and Evaluation Squadron following the disbanding of the Fast Jet Test Squadron at Boscombe Down.

The final scheme to be presented on the unit's Tornado F.3s came in 2002 when the insignia was reduced in size and portrayed on a red disc mounted centrally on the fin. ZE168 'UN' and ZH554 are seen here in April 2002 en route from Eglin AFB, Florida, to Bangor, Maine, on the first leg of the transit back to the UK following ASRAAM missile trails over the Gulf of Mexico. ZE168 had by this time adopted the 'new' coding system but ZH554 never did so whilst with the OEU.

OC No.111 Squadron Wing Commander Rob Birch and OC F3OEU Wing Commander Robin Birtwistle seen at RAF Leuchars at the service introduction of ASRAAM in September 2002. The F3OEU undertook most of the service trials of this missile before it was certified for use by the front-line units.

UNIT MARKINGS

The insignia of the Strike Command's CTTO was applied to the mid-fin of the unit's aircraft, the badge consisting of a pale blue ring on which were placed three red swords joined at the hilt and pointing outwards. No codes were carried by the aircraft at this stage.

August 1994 saw the OEU parented by the newly formed Air Warfare Centre (AWC) at RAF Waddington. ZE889 became the first of the unit's jets to receive a redesigned tail marking comprising a red chevron with the letters AWC in a central white disc. This aircraft also received the tail code 'SB' after the officer commanding, Stuart Black. By early 1996 the markings were revised once more with commonality between the two elements of the AWC. The old F3OEU retained its red chevron but the AWC letters were done away with and replaced with a three-winged sword. In March 2004 the F3OEU became part of the Fast Jet Weapon Operational Evaluation Unit (FJWOEU) incorporating both the SAOEU and the AGWOEU and the tail marking was redesigned to reflect this change with the chevron being replaced by a disc but still containing the three-winged sword.

This was later changed in 2006 to No.41 [R] Squadron markings as the FJWOEU took shadow squadron status thus preserving one the RAF's dwindling number of squadrons.

Tornado F.3 ZE168 became, it is believed, the only Tornado F.3 to achieve an air-to-air kill. During the missile trials in the United States the jet successfully shot down two QF-4E drones and in true RAF tradition gained suitable kill markings just below the cockpit. The jet is seen on the ramp at Bangor, Maine, prior to the leg to Lajes in the Azores.

ZG731, depicted here in formation with VC.10K2 ZA142 'C' of No.101 Squadron, spent over seven years as part of the trials fleet with BAE Systems at Warton, the FJ&WOEU and finally No.41 [Reserve] Squadron at RAF Coningsby. It was finally pensioned off on 24 June 2009 when it was flown to Leeming to be reduced to produce.

Although operating with No.25 Squadron at the time during Exercise Indradhanush, ZG731 sports the marking of No.41 [Reserve] Squadron. The squadron did not relinquish its development of F.3 systems and tactics until December 2007 when the last aircraft was delivered to RAF Leuchars.

CHAPTER 5

NO.5 SQUADRON

NO.5 SQUADRON was the third RAF squadron to convert to the Panavia Tornado F.3 receiving its first aircraft, ZE292, on 27 September 1987 when still No.5 (designate) Squadron having previously flown the English Electric Lightning F6. It stood down on the Lightning at the end of October that year, standing up on 1 January 1988 with the Tornado F.3 and undertaking its first month-long armament practice camp (APC) at RAF Akrotiri on 12 July 1988. The unit attended Red Flag exercise 96/3 at Nellis AFB in January 1993, taking with them six aeroplanes drawn jointly from both RAF Coningsby front-line units; No.29 Squadron bringing the aircraft home again.

No.5 Squadron was the second front-line squadron to equip with the Tornado F.3, being declared operational in the spring of 1988. At the time it had really high visibility markings as shown in this shot of ZE755 'CG' landing at RAF Coningsby on 17 March 1988. These were, however, relatively short-lived as the squadron sanitised its aircraft before deploying to Saudi Arabia just under two years later as part of Operation Desert Shield.

Post-Operation Granby markings failed to return to their former glory partly because of the continued swapping of airframes to meet operational commitments caused by Deny Flight, Operations Resinate and Bolton and the like, even though it was only the stage 1+ aircraft that actually deployed. It therefore became very difficult to accurately identify the users of particular airframes; something that did not stabilise until only the Leuchars wing were operating the aeroplane. Here in this BAe shot, ZE254 'CA' and ZG730 'CC' of No.5 Squadron have only the Maple Leaf with a Roman five superimposed at the top of the fin.

Uncoded 5 Squadron marked ZE788, seen here in company with ZG778 'BG' 29 Squadron on 15 July 1999, operating as part of a four-ship mission with ZE966 'DX' of XI Squadron and a totally unmarked aircraft using call-signs 'Razor 1 to 4', highlighting the difficulty of identifying ownership of units when the F.3 was in such a state of flux.

In October 1992 No.5 Squadron spearheaded an RAF Coningsby deployment to Red Flag 93/1. Once again for the deployment the RAF sent predominantly Leeming-assigned stage 1+ aircraft rather than the attending squadron's own jets, the Leeming aircraft being of the higher modification state.

One of the RAF's first front-line squadrons, No.5 formed at Farnborough on 26 July 1913. The squadron then went to France to provide reconnaissance for the BEF in August 1914. The squadron had the distinction of recording the RFCs first war casualties when an aircraft was hit by rifle fire on 22 August 1914. The squadron then took a leading role in the development of aerial photography and wireless telephony during the early days of the war. Artillery observation was the main task with BE2Cs and in 1917 the squadron formed a close association with the Canadian Corps, remaining with them after the Armistice as part of the Army of Occupation in Germany. In 1920 the squadron re-formed at Quetta, India, for army co-operation work on the North West Frontier. Its venerable Bristol Fighters remained with them for eleven years until replaced in 1931 by Wapitis. These outdated biplanes unbelievably remained until 1940 when they where replaced by equally ancient Hawker Harts!

In 1942 Mohawk fighters arrived and the aircraft moved to Assam and escorted Bristol Blenheims attacking targets in North West Burma. Subsequent types flown included Hurricanes and Thunderbolts before, in 1947, the squadron was disbanded. On 11 February 1949, it was re-formed at Pembrey in South Wales on mundane target-towing duties. In September 1951, No.5 Squadron moved to Germany and flew de Havilland Vampires and Venom

fighter-bombers before succumbing to defence cuts in 1957. During 1959 it was reborn as part of the all-weather fighter force in Germany, flying Gloster Javelins, and moved to RAF Binbrook in 1965 with the all-new EE Lightning F6. These remained the

No.5 Squadron crewing in for the start of a Red Flag sortie at Nellis AFB, Nevada, during October 1992.

Tornado F.3 ZE839 'CH' of No.5 Squadron operating over the North Sea off Newcastle as 'Scorpion 2' on 5 September 2000. This was the squadron's final set of markings before the unit disbanded on 27 September 2002.

A No.5 Squadron crew take off from Nellis AFB main runway during Red Flag 93/1. The jet is ZE763 'BA' of No.29 Squadron, one of six aircraft deployed to the Nevada base. The F.3 squadrons had to rely on exceptional training, guile and some wacky tactics to have any chance of dominating against the sophisticated assets they were to come up against during a Red Flag exercise. The Foxhunter radar, even with improvements, was fundamentally unsuited to dogfight engagements. It would be only the introduction of Link-16 or JTIDS, plus better missile technology, that would allow the Tornado F.3 to hold its own and even then only by choosing to fight on its own terms.

Later the red bars were to return, as depicted on ZG735 'CO' and ZG730 'CC' for this BAe/British Airways publicity shot. Both the jets depicted, as with all jets of No.5 Squadron, were fitted with stage 1 AI.24 Foxhunter radars. Both aircraft later became part of the loan package to Italy and neither was to return to RAF service.

squadron's mount until 1987, when these were replaced by the Panavia Tornado F.3, and it moved to RAF Coningsby. A combined 5/29 Squadron was the first RAF component to arrive in Saudi Arabia in August 1990 after the Iraqi invasion of Kuwait.

Its time at RAF Coningsby as part of the No.11 Group air defence structure was very limited. In October 2002 No.5 Squadron disbanded at RAF Coningsby prior to later re-forming at RAF Waddington where it now operates the Sentinel R.1 and Shadow

R.1 aircraft. The farewell flypast took place on 26 September with six aircraft comprising ZE164/UQ, ZE968/XB, ZE342/YS, ZE162/UR, ZE758/YI and ZE203 as call-sign 'Scorpion 1 to 6' with four of the jets recovering to RAF Leeming for use by that wing's squadrons.

However, in the short period of Tornado F.3 operation the squadron won the Seed Trophy for gunnery in 1989 and 1990 and deployed to the Royal Malayan air base at Butterworth for the

By 1996 the red nose markings had returned as seen on ZG796 'CE', call-sign 'Barrel 1', as it takes on fuel from VC.10K3 ZA150, 'Tartan 34', in refuelling area 5 on 15 May 1996.

ADEX 90-2 air defence exercise. The unit markings were also to vary quite considerably over the short five-year tenure of Tornado F.3 operation.

UNIT MARKINGS

After several trials in 1987, the unit adopted a red band (edged in dark green) applied horizontally across the fin upon which was the squadron's maple leaf emblem in a white disc. A red arrowhead was applied to the forward fuselage, on which was placed the toned-down Type B roundel. Squadron codes, in the 'Cx' range, were in white and placed under the fin markings.

Early 1991 saw a change to these marks, with the deletion of the red fin and nose flashes. Atop the fin was the maple leaf, this time with a gold roman numeral 'V' surmounting it. By the end of that year, however, red bars had been applied on either side of that marking, the unit coding remaining unchanged.

By early 1996 a red chevron had been re-applied to the nose either side of the roundel though by 1998 these had been removed and the roman numeral 'V' replaced by a stylised '5'. A green Maple Leaf emblem with a roman numeral 'V' superimposed upon it had been positioned centrally on the fin. By 1999 this had been removed from most airframes, whilst the individual aircraft code, still in the 'Cx' range, had been repositioned to the trailing edge of the fin within the red band. These were in grey. Ultimately unit codes were altered to represent individual airframes but before this really took hold the squadron disbanded.

CHAPTER 6

NO.29 SQUADRON

NO.29 SQUADRON was the first front-line RAF squadron to equip with the Tornado F.3, officially re-forming on the type on 1 April 1987.

Transition to the ADV variant of the Tornado began in December 1986 with the first cadre of crews beginning training with 229 OCU, although some of these were already conversant with the Tornado having transferred from the IDS version. The RAF had wisely cross-trained some of its former air defence pilots onto the Tornado IDS with a view to providing an easily available selection of former air defenders with tornado experience.

As the RAF's flagship on the Tornado F.3, the squadron undertook a number of high-profile tasks in its early years with four aircraft participating in Operation Golden Eagle where the jets and crews circumnavigated the world. En route they participated in Malaysian and Thai air defence exercises and in airshows in Australia and the United States.

Declared as a SACLANT asset with additional out-of-area commitments, the unit had a high profile. Initially formed at Gosport on 7 November 1915 from a nucleus supplied by No.23 Squadron, after training the unit moved to France in March 1916 as the third squadron to be fully equipped with fighters. Its DH2s were engaged in escort duties to protect the slow and vulnerable reconnaissance aircraft over the Western Front, achieving their first combat victory on 1 May 1916. In March 1917 it re-equipped with Nieuport Scouts, and in April 1918 these were replaced by SE5As, which were used for the rest of the war on fighter and ground-attack missions. After a short period in Germany, the squadron was reduced to a cadre and in August 1919 returned to RAF Spittlegate in the UK, where it was disbanded on 31 December 1919.

On 1 April 1923 No.29 re-formed as a fighter squadron at RAF Duxford with Snipes, re-equipping with Grebes in January 1925. In turn, these were replaced by Siskins in March 1928 and Bulldogs in June 1932. In March 1935, No.29 became a two-seat fighter

squadron with the arrival of Hawker Demons, which it took in October to Egypt during the Abyssinian crisis, a few Gordons being used for night patrols at this time. Returning to the UK a year later, it converted to Bristol Blenheims in the December of 1938. At the outbreak of the Second World War these were used for patrols over shipping and for early trials with airborne radar. When German night bombers began operating in strength in June 1940, No.29 became fully involved in night-fighting, beginning to receive Bristol Beaufighters in the November, though it was February 1941 before the squadron was fully equipped. Its defensive role remained after conversion to de Havilland Mosquitoes in May 1943, but in May 1944 intruder missions began to be flown which and continued until February 1945. Conversion to DH Mosquito 30s followed, but few operations with these were flown before the end of the war. In October 1945 the squadron moved to RAF

No.29 Squadron, although being the first front-line user of the Tornado F.3 and operating the aircraft for over ten years, never changed its markings. ZG774 'BE' seen landing at Coningsby in 1995 had already seen service with both No.43 (F) Squadron and No.65 (Shadow) Squadron by the time it was taken on strength with No.29 Squadron.

In factory-fresh condition, having only been delivered to the RAF three months previously, Tornado F.3 ZH553 'BY' of 29 Squadron is seen departing RAF Marham on 2 April 1993 following the Royal Review. The squadron carried the flag for the RAF and the Tornado fleet in its early years, having been the first front-line squadron to equip with the type. Its sixty-six-day round the world tour beginning in August 1988 saw the unit visit Oman, Malaysia (where it participated in Exercise Lima Bersatu 88), and Richmond, Australia, for the bicentennial celebrations.

West Malling to become part of the peacetime night-fighter force in the UK.

The DH Mosquitoes continued to serve until replaced by Gloster Meteors in August 1951 at RAF Tangmere. In January 1957 the squadron moved north, first to Northumberland and then in July 1958 to Scotland, conversion to Gloster Javelins having taken place in November 1957. In February 1963, No.29 was moved to Cyprus and in December 1965 went to Zambia for nine months on detachment during the Rhodesian crisis. In May 1967 the squadron returned to the UK to become part of the No.11 Group

air defence structure, re-equipping with EE Lightning F.3s before once again disbanding on 31 December 1974. No.29 re-formed at RAF Coningsby as a Phantom FGR.2 squadron on 1 January 1975. A detachment was provided for the defence of the Falklands as soon as the airfield at Stanley was capable of operating Phantoms at the end of August 1982. This became No.23 Squadron in March 1983.

The squadron swapped its Phantom FGR.2s for Tornado F.3 fighters in 1987. No.29 Squadron became the first operational squadron to be equipped with the Tornado F.3, deploying to Saudi

No.360 Squadron at RAF Wyton with it 'EW' Canberra T.17A was in high demand during the early years of the Tornado F.3, when crews were attempting to get used to the complexities of the Foxhunter AI radar. Here a pair of No.29 Squadron F.3s, ZE165 'BJ' and ZG733 'BK' formate, on No.360 Squadron's 25th anniversary schemed Canberra WD955 flown by Flight Lieutenant Rory Underwood on 18 December 1991 prior to a 'Magic' exercise.

Arabia after the Iraqi invasion of Kuwait in August 1990 and flying throughout Operation Desert Storm in the air defence role. It undertook its first armament practice camp (APC) at RAF Akrotiri in March 1989 and it was from such a deployment the following year that it became one of the first units to deploy as part of Operation Desert Shield. The squadron was again disbanded in October 1998 before re-forming once again, this time as the Eurofighter Typhoon Operational Conversion Unit.

UNIT MARKINGS

The insignia of an eagle (red) in flight, preying on a buzzard (gold) adorns the centre of the fin, with codes finished in red (in the 'Bx' sequence) situated atop the fin. The nose roundel is located below the cockpit. The forward marking, consisting of three 'X's between two lines, all finished in red and edged in gold, is applied diagonally to the lip of the air intakes.

CHAPTER 7

RAF LEEMING

THE SITE NOW occupied by RAF Leeming was originally developed during the late 1930s. Leeming has been used as a heavy bomber base, night-fighter base and a Flying Training School, before it underwent major redevelopment in the mid-1980s. Currently Hawk T.1 aircraft of No.100 Squadron and Tutor aircraft (Northumbrian University Air Squadron) operate from Leeming. In addition, No.34 Squadron RAF Regiment and No.609 (West Riding) RAF Auxiliary Squadron are resident on the station. Two further small units are located on the unit, namely No.2 Tactical Survive to Operate (2 TacSTO) and the Joint Forward Air Controller Training and Standards Unit (JFACTSU). RAF Leeming also accommodates No.10 Royal Engineers Field Squadron and the Expeditionary Radar Airfield Squadron.

The Tornado F.3 arrived at RAF Leeming on 1 July 1988 when No.XI [F] Squadron arrived from RAF Coningsby following conversion. The aircraft were to form part of the UK's Immediate Rapid Reaction Force (Air), and as such some aircraft could expect to be deployed anywhere in the world within 48 hours. In addition, the station had the Quick Reaction Alert (Interceptor) commitment for both Southern and Northern Q as stations converted to new types.

No.XI Squadron was followed into RAF Leeming by No.23 Squadron on 5 August 1988 and by No.25 Squadron on 1 October 1989. In 1994 the station provided a sixteen-aircraft formation for HM the Queen's Birthday Flypast. However, following the drawdown of the Panavia Tornado F.3 force, all of the RAF Leeming front-line squadrons have since disbanded, although the station still plays a pivotal role in the F.3 story.

Today it has the responsibility of reclaiming Tornado F.3s and then shipping their carcasses out to scrap. Aircraft are now brought into Leeming, either by air or road, for dismantling. There is, however, only one 'RTP Jig' and it takes on average eighteen working days to strip components from the jet for recycling before the airframe can be disposed of. Currently there are a number of aircraft stored on the station awaiting this fate.

Silhouetted against the morning sky, a pair of Tornado F.3 aircraft carry out a simulated Air Defence Patrol.

CHAPTER 8

NO.11 SQUADRON

NO.11 SQUADRON became the first of the 'new' Leeming Wing squadrons to be equipped with the Panavia Tornado F.3. A former Lightning operator, it was no stranger to the air defence role – neither was its first Tornado F.3 Commanding Officer, Wing Commander David Hamilton, who had served on both the Lightning with Nos 5 and 23 Squadrons and the Phantom FGR.2 and FG.1 with Nos 92 and 892 Squadrons.

The squadron received its first aircraft on 25 April 1988 when still No.11 (designate) Squadron. It officially re-formed on 1 July 1988 having stood down on the Lightning at RAF Binbrook on 30 April.

The squadron became the lead unit with Tornado F.3 Stage 1+ aircraft for Operation Granby when it deployed with a composite squadron comprising of some eighteen aircraft. It again became the lead squadron when the RAF deployed Tornado F.3s to Gioia

In the latter days of the English Electric Lightning the aircraft received coloured tails. No.5 Squadron's were all red and No.XI Squadron's black. The charismatic Wing Commander David Hamilton, upon taking command of No.XI Squadron with the Tornado F.3, had his personal mount, ZE764 'DH', suitably adorned to carry on the tradition. This was relatively short-lived with the arrival of the Gulf War, although it has in latter days returned to some degree to maintain that *esprit de corps* and moral.

No.XI Squadron were SACLANT-assigned and as such a deployable asset. The assigned hardened aircraft shelters (HAS), as with the Jaguar force, were therefore elsewhere and in the case of the two SACLANT-assigned Tornado F.3 units these were at Stornoway in northern Scotland and St Mawgan in Cornwall. Therefore when home-based the aircraft operated from a flight line as seen here at RAF Leeming in February 1989.

del Colle in April 1993 as part of Operation Clear Skies, later to become Operation Deny Flight. The squadron was later to trial the SEAD role with the fitting of ALARM missiles.

Formed at Netheravon on 14 February 1915 from a nucleus provided by No.7 Squadron, No.11 Squadron claims to be the first RFC unit specifically equipped as a scout unit. By the time the squadron moved to St Omer, France, in July, it was equipped with the Vickers 'Gunbus' and was quickly pressed into action. In November Second Lieutenant GSM Insall was awarded the VC. Having forced down an Aviatik and destroyed it with a well-aimed incendiary bomb, his aircraft was then damaged by ground fire.

After force landing the aircraft, Insall and his observer/gunner repaired a fuel leak and flew back to base the following morning.

In May 1917, the squadron became involved in offensive patrols, and joined the Army of Occupation after the Armistice, returning to the UK in late 1919 prior to disbanding shortly afterwards. Re-formed at Andover in January 1923, the squadron spent short periods on communications and day bombing duties before moving to Risalpur, India (now Pakistan), and equipping with Westland Wapitis and then a modified version of the Hawker Hart bomber. By the time war broke out in 1939, the squadron had received Bristol Blenheims, and was transferred to Aden at the outset of the East Africa campaign. Following action in a variety of operations, No.11 Squadron moved to Colombo, Ceylon (now Sri Lanka), in early 1942 and was involved in a number of unsuccessful attacks on Japanese ships. During 1943, the squadron moved to Burma (now Myanmar) and used its newly arrived Hurricane ground-attack aircraft in support of the XIVth Army. With the surrender of Japan in August 1945, the squadron moved to Japan as part of the Commonwealth occupation forces, remaining there until disbanded in February 1948.

Re-formed in Germany during October 1949, the squadron spent several short periods with fighters of the period (DH Mosquitos, Vampires and Venoms) until again disbanding during 1957, only to re-form yet again in January 1959 with Gloster Meteor night-fighters. Three years later, Gloster Javelins replaced the Meteors and these remained on strength until once again No.11 Squadron was disbanded in 1966. Re-forming in early 1967 with EE Lightnings, the squadron spent the next seventeen years flying this aircraft, until disbanding in May 1988, prior to re-forming at RAF Leeming three months later with the Tornado F.3. In October 2005, after another period of seventeen years, the squadron once again disbanded. It later re-equipped with the Eurofighter Typhoon at RAF Coningsby.

UNIT MARKINGS

Taken from the squadron's crest, 'two eagles volant in pale' are applied in the centre of the fin, on top of which is the squadron code ('Dx' range) in black, edged in gold. The nose roundel is superimposed on a black rectangle, with yellow triangles to each side of the roundel. The Commanding Officer's mount coded 'DH' with black spine and tail.

Markings altered in 1999 with the nose-bars being relocated to the fin tip and the double eagle on the tail fin being reduced in size but superimposed on a yellow background. The first aircraft so painted was ZE160/DV.

No.XI Squadron's first two Tornado F.3s, ZE785 'DA' and ZE787 'DB', seen during work-up over the North Sea on 6 July 1988. By this period the squadron had eight of its assigned twelve aircraft.

In perfect formation, ZE295 'DC' and ZE763 'DG' wait their turn to refuel off Tristar KC.1 ZD949 on 23 June 2005 whilst operating with No.XI Squadron. The two jets have a variation in markings with ZE763 having already lost the nose-bars. That particular aircraft undertook ALARM trials in April 2003 when consideration was given to finding the F.3 force, or part of it, an additional role. Ultimately the SEAD role has remained to domain of the Tornado GR.4 force.

Silhouetted against the North Sea is ZE942 'DF' in No.XI Squadron colours. The jet was being operated by No.111 Squadron as part of 'Adept 11 Flight' during Exercise Wycombe Warrior. The squadron refuelled twice from VC.10C.1K XV109 'Z' on both refuelling area 5 and area 8 on 3 October 2006.

The black tail became synonymous with No.XI Squadron and ZE887, appropriately coded 'XI', received this attractive scheme to mark the squadron's 90th anniversary. It is seen here at the 2005 Royal International Air Tattoo at RAF Fairford. The aircraft has since retained its black fin and received similar appropriate marks from other squadrons.

Another classic case of who operates what. ZE942 in No.XI Squadron markings alongside a pair of Tornado F.3s from No.111 Squadron. All three jets were being operated by the latter squadron and were seen during Exercise Wycombe Warrior on 3 October 2006. ZE942 had first been noted operating with the Leuchars-based squadron during the previous November, with whom it remained until withdrawn from use (wfu) in August 2007 after suffering a bird strike in the May that was deemed not cost-effective to repair.

Clean with a full missile fit including both AIM-9 Sidewinder and ASRAAM, ZE294 'DD' of No.XI Squadron is seen making a racy departure from RAF Fairford during July 2004 following participation in the Air Tattoo. This aircraft was one of the Tornado F.3s to have suffered damage whilst on overhaul at St Athan in 1995. It was later to receive the centre fuselage section from F.2 ZD906 before re-entering service with No.111 Squadron.

CHAPTER 9

NO.23 SQUADRON

NO.23 SQUADRON became the second of the Leeming Wing squadrons and its first casualty. It formed on the Panavia Tornado F.3 on 1 November 1988 at RAF Leeming when the four aircraft detachment of Phantom FGR.2s at RAF Stanley were renumbered 1435 Flight. Its first aircraft was taken on charge on 5 August 1988 prior to officially re-forming.

Seen at RAF Leeming shortly after delivery, Tornado F.3 ZE832 'EB' taxis out from the squadron's HAS area. The jet saw only limited service with the RAF but having the stage 1 AI.24 Foxhunter radar it found its way into the AMI loan programme and was delivered to Italy on 4 July 1995 as MM7202/36-12. It returned from lease on 26 April 2003 to St Athan where it was wfu and recovered for spares.

When the RAF decided to participate in Exercise Distant Frontier 92 in Alaska it needed to find aircraft with the stage 1 AI.24 radars and ones that had oil-efficient engines for the long transit legs. Although the deployment would be an all-111 Squadron affair, the six aircraft involved were all drawn from the Leeming Wing. Four were taken from No.25 Squadron and two from No.23 Squadron. ZE936 'EE', ZE808 'FA' and ZE206 'EW' are seen here during the final leg from CFB Goose Bay, Labrador to Eielson AFB, Fairbanks, Alaska.

Exercise Distant Frontier 92 turned out to be a true test for both the aircraft and the crews whilst at Eielson AFB. A freak cold front sent temperatures down to significantly below zero, at the same time dumping copious amounts of snow on the aircraft that had to be left outside. The intense cold soak saw all bar one aircraft go unserviceable on the first operating day as seals perished and plastic switches snapped. Full credit to the ground engineers, however, that the second saw a full compliment serviceable.

The squadron originally formed at Fort Grange, Gosport on 1 September 1915 under the command of one of the RAF's most experienced operational pilots, Captain Louis Strange. After a brief period attempting to counter German airship flights over London, the squadron moved to France with its FE2Bs initially employed on escort duties. By early 1917, Spad single-seaters had arrived, and were being used on offensive patrols. By the end of the war, the squadron had converted to Dolphins, and flew these until disbanded at the end of 1919.

On 1 July 1925, No.23 Squadron re-formed at RAF Henlow with Sopwith Snipes, but these were replaced shortly after with Gloster Gamecocks. In 1931 the squadron was tasked with carrying out trials on the new Hawker Hart two-seaters, taking the production version, known as Demons, on strength in 1933. It wasn't until late 1938 that the squadron received its first monoplanes in the form of Bristol Blenheims, and these were used as night-fighters in the early days of the Second World War whilst based at RAF Wittering. In 1941, Douglas Havocs replaced the Blenheims, and these were used with great success in the intruder role until they themselves were replaced by the de Havilland Mosquito in mid-1942. At the end of the year, the squadron moved to Malta in support of Allied operations in the Mediterranean before returning to the UK in 1944.

In September 1945, the squadron had disbanded, re-forming a year later at RAF Wittering with Mosquito night-fighters. By late 1953, DH Venom night-fighters had joined the squadron, before Gloster Javelin all-weather supersonic fighters replaced these in 1957. In 1964, the EE Lightning F6 replaced the Javelin, and it was with this classic aircraft that the squadron continued at RAF Leuchars until Phantom FGR.2s were received in late 1975, this coinciding with a move to RAF Wattisham in Suffolk. After the Falklands War in 1982, the squadron occupied Port Stanley airfield until reduced to a flight of four aircraft in 1988, re-forming at Leeming with Tornado F.3s. The squadron had the misfortune to suffer the very first Tornado F.3 loss when ZE833/EC crashed some 30 miles north-east of Newcastle during June 1989.

In 1992 the squadron undertook a long-distance deployment to Malaysia in support of the IADS 92 exercise, taking with them six aircraft, ZE969/EA, ZE168/EB, ZE936/EE, ZE159/EG, ZE206/EW and ZE983/EZ. Defence cuts following the end of the Cold War and the 'Options for Change' review saw the unit disbanded

on 28 February 1994, the announcement having been made on 7 July 1993 whilst the squadron was undertaking Deny Flight duties at Gioia del Colle in Italy.

The resident USAF squadron operated from flow-through barns and thus avoided much of the cold-induced serviceability problems. Those that didn't live under cover generally formed the second wave of flying after they had thawed slowly. Here 111 Squadron ground crews attempt to keep the jets de-iced.

UNIT MARKINGS

The unit's red eagle emblem, swooping as if to capture prey, is located centre-fin. Unit codes in white (in the 'Ex' range) were applied to the upper fin. The nose roundel was placed upon an arrowhead of red and blue chevrons.

CHAPTER 10

NO.25 SQUADRON

This somewhat pacy departure from RAF Fairford of ZE961/XD graphically illustrates the forward motion of the undercarriage when retracting. The aircraft when delivered to the RAF in 1989 became the first mount for No.43 Squadron at RAF Leuchars. Today it is one of a handful of jets still active.

THE THIRD LEEMING Wing squadron, No.25, was to be the last Tornado F.3 squadron at the Yorkshire base when the UK Air Defence structure was reduced to just two operating locations.

Because the Panavia Tornado F.3 originally represented part of a strengthening of No.11 Group, some of the Tornado squadrons were new units. No.25 Squadron represented one of these; the other being No.23 Squadron. When it was announced that the squadron would be the third Leeming squadron to receive the Panavia Tornado F.3 it was still technically 'on the books' as a Bloodhound SAM Squadron and therefore already part of the air defence structure.

Sporting a special anniversary colour scheme, ZE167 belonging to No.25 Squadron is seen landing at RAF Fairford in July 1991. The aircraft later became part of the Italian lease deal and with 53 Stormo received the unit's famous tiger colour scheme. The jet, however, returned to UK charge on 31 March 2004 and following spares recovery had been scrapped by the end of the year.

Leading this four-ship of Tornado F.3s is ZE210 of No.25 Squadron flown by OC No.111 Squadron Wing Commander Pete Walker. The jets were en route to Alaska for Exercise Distant Frontier 92. This particular aircraft, however, was subject to a mid-air collision with ZE733 on 30 October 1995 and, although recovered and initially considered CAT 3 or possibly CAT 4 damage, it was eventually struck off charge as beyond economical repair. It remained in storage at St Athan for a number of years before being finally disposed of in January 2001.

Caught against a setting sun between layers of cloud are a three-ship of No.25 Squadron Tornado F.3s. The squadron went on to become the last of the Leeming squadrons to operate the jet before disbanding on 4 April 2008.

Formed as No.25 (designate) Squadron at RAF Leeming on 1 July 1989 it became officially established on 1 October immediately following the SAM Bloodhound Squadron disbanding. The squadron received its first aircraft on 15 December 1988 but it was seven months before it was to receive more. The unit was declared to NATO on 1 January 1990.

As part of the Leeming Wing the squadron became equipped with the Stage 1+ aircraft and was at the forefront of operational deployments, participating in Deny Flight operations from Gioia del Colle in Italy from September 1993, Operation Decisive Edge in 1996 and later hosting the Indian Air Force for Exercise Indradhanush at RAF Waddington.

No.25 Squadron was originally formed at Montrose in Scotland on 25 September 1915 from the personnel of No.6 Reserve Squadron. Moving to France in February 1916, the squadron took up fighter/reconnaissance patrols over the Western Front with two-seat FE2Bs. During 1917, the squadron transferred to long-range reconnaissance and high-altitude bombing with

Shot over the North Sea on refuelling area 6 on 13 October 1998, this three-ship was presumably being operated by No.25 Squadron even though the number two aircraft, ZE200/DB, was in No.XI Squadron markings. That said, the jet was on No.5 Squadron strength the following month. ZE165/ZK on the other hand sports a non-standard set of unit markings with the nose-bars not generally adopted in the squadron.

newly received DH4s. After moving to Germany as part of the occupation forces, No.25 Squadron returned to the UK and disbanded in January 1920.

The squadron re-formed at RAF Hawkinge three months later and at this time No.25 was the only home-based fighter unit! With the exception of a ten-month detachment to Turkey during the Chanak crisis of 1922–23, No.25 Squadron spent the inter-war years at Hawkinge with various fighters including Grebes, Siskins and Demons. The squadron moved to RAF Northolt in August 1939 and began night patrols with Bristol Blenheims, before assuming convoy protection duties in 1940. In 1942, after briefly flying Bristol Beaufighters, Westland Whirlwinds and Douglas Havocs, DH Mosquitos were employed on intruder flights and

night-fighter patrols with occasional bomber escort duties. By the end of the Second World War, the squadron was almost exclusively flying bomber support missions.

After the war, the night-fighter Mosquitos remained on strength until 1951 when they were finally replaced by DH Vampires. A mix of two Gloster Meteor night-fighter variants replaced the Vampires in 1954 and remained with the squadron until it was disbanded in June 1958. Barely a week later, on 1 July 1958, No.153 Squadron at RAF Waterbeach was renumbered No.25 and the same mix of Meteors (NF12s and NF14s) was flown until all-weather Gloster Javelin fighters arrived in early 1959. In November 1962, the squadron again disbanded, this time until October 1963, when the squadron was re-formed at RAF North Coates as the first

Showing its clear lineage, a No.25 Squadron Tornado F.3 enters formation alongside its stubbier GR.4A cousin.

ZE887/FX still sporting its black tail from its former XI Squadron days is seen taking off from RAF Waddington during Exercise Indradhanush. The aircraft was later to receive the squadron's 90th anniversary markings along with ZG780 (depicted below).

No.25 Squadron celebrated its 90th anniversary in 2005 and painted two aircraft into a very attractive commemorative scheme, ZE887 as described earlier, and ZG780, depicted here captured low level over Thirlmere Lake in northern England on 9 August 2007. The anniversary markings were later altered to reflect the unit's disbandment in 2008.

With heat haze behind, clean configured ZE254/FD of No.25 Squadron rolls to a slow taxi pace at the end of RAF Waddington's runway during Exercise Indradhanush in 2007. Following the disbandment of the squadron, the aircraft was transferred to RAF Leuchars for use by No.43 Squadron until it was flown back to RAF Leeming for RTP on 29 August 2008. During the exercise, the Tornado F.3s gave good account of themselves when up against the formidable Indian Air Force Sukhoi Su-30MKI 'Flanker' aircraft. However, as the Indians were restricted from using their radars, the RAF, with the aid of JTIDS, could hardly fail.

operational Bloodhound surface-to-air guided missile unit. In 1970, the squadron moved to RAF Bruggen with detached flights based at RAF Laarbruch and RAF Wildenrath, remaining in Germany until 1983 when the unit returned to the UK with bases at RAF Wyton, Barkston Heath and Wattisham. The Bloodhounds were withdrawn from service on 1 August 1989 and the squadron re-formed the same day at Leeming as a Tornado F.3 squadron.

No.25 Squadron, as the last RAF Leeming-based Tornado F.3 squadron, disbanded on 4 April 2008.

UNIT MARKINGS

'On a gauntlet a hawk rising affrontee' is the heraldic term for the squadron's insignia applied to the middle of the fin. Across the top of the fin is a horizontal band of silver, edged in black. Codes, in the 'Fx' range, are in white with black edging and are applied to the fin's trailing edge atop the rudder. No nose markings are worn, the roundel being situated on the air intake. Markings were later toned down with a smaller version of the Hawk emblem on the fin.

Low-level flying when there is moisture in the air can produce quite dynamic effects. Wing tip vortices are quite common as depicted in this shot of ZE969/FH as it pulls hard to navigate the Bwlch pass in the Machynlleth Loop on 27 March 2008.

The beauty of the podded system on the RAFs VC.10 tankers is the ability to refuel two jets simultaneously. Here on the starboard station of ZA147 Tornado F.3 ZE342/FG can be seen 'plugged in' and taking on fuel whilst still in the turn. Again this is very demanding flying, although I am assured that once you 'get the hang of it' the process is quite simple. ZE342, as will be noted, is in a revised darker grey colour scheme with full colour national insignia. This scheme was only applied to a very few Tornado F.3s and was captured here on refuelling area 5 between Flamborough Head and Newcastle on 20 July 2007 whilst operating as 'Savage 4' in company with ZE201, ZE794 and ZE728, the latter jet to become a bit of a celebrity in its afterlife.

HM the Queen's 2007 Birthday Flypast saw No.25 Squadron have the honour of representing the Tornado F.3 force. Here, in company with No.101 Squadron VC.10K3 ZA150, the formation is seen overhead RAF Marham during a rehearsal on 13 June and although neat and to some degree quite tame I am assured by those that had to fly in close formation for a sustained period that it is very demanding.

Exercise Indradhanush was considered a major benefit to both RAF and IAF assets alike. Here, in this BAe publicity picture, in perfect formation are a No.25 Squadron Tornado F.3, a Typhoon F.2 from No.17 Squadron and a Su-30MKI from No.20 Squadron IAF at Pune. Such were the advances in the AI.24 radar of the Tornado along with the application of JTIDS and much-improved missile technology that the Tornado could be a match for even the most versatile of next-generation fighter, providing it was on its own terms.

CHAPTER 11

RAF LEUCHARS

THE FIRST OPERATIONAL Panavia Tornado F.3 to arrive at RAF Leuchars occurred on 1 October 1989 when ZE961/GA and ZE962/GB arrived for the newly re-formed No.43 Squadron. Today the station is the last remaining frontline F.3 operator in the United Kingdom.

Aviation at Leuchars dates back to 1911 with a balloon squadron of the Royal Engineers setting up a training camp in Tentsmuir Forest. They were soon joined in the skies by the 'string and sealing wax' aircraft of the embryonic Royal Flying Corps; such aircraft favoured the sands of St Andrews, where not the least of the attractions was the availability of fuel from local garages.

Like so many RAF stations, the airfield itself owes its existence to the hot stimulus of war, and work began on levelling the existing site on Reres Farm in 1916. From the beginning, Leuchars was intended as a training unit, being termed a 'Temporary Mobilisation Station' taking aspiring aircrew from initial flying training through to fleet co-operation work. Building was still under way when the Armistice was signed in 1918. Most was made of Leuchars' maritime location when it was designated a Naval Fleet Training School, eventually to undertake the training of 'naval spotting' crews who acted as eyes for the Royal Navy's capital ships.

The unit was formally named 'Royal Air Force Leuchars' in March 1920, but nevertheless retained its strong naval links.

As the Navy embraced the value of aviation, the aircraft carrier was added to its inventory. Many of the flights 'dedicated' to Leuchars were detached to such vessels for months at a time, with light and dark blue uniforms apparently mixing happily together. At St Andrews, the citizens were not unaware of the potential use of aviation and attempts were made to use aircraft as a means of transport for golfing enthusiasts. More successful were the barn-storming displays of the flying circuses which were extremely popular in the city.

In 1935 Leuchars became home to No.1 Flying Training School (No.1 FTS) and ranges for practice bombing were established in Tentsmuir Forest. As the war clouds gathered over Europe its maritime position ensured that Leuchars would come to enjoy a more warlike role. No.1 FTS moved to Netheravon and the station came under the control of Coastal Command. With the arrival of Nos 224 and 233 Squadrons in August 1938 the station enjoyed an operational rather than training role for the first time.

On the second day of the war a Hudson of No.224 Squadron attacked a Dornier 18 over the North Sea with inconclusive results but became the first British aircraft to engage the enemy in the Second World War. Leuchars was not to secure the romantic image of a Battle of Britain station but rather settled to the routine of hour upon hour of maritime patrol. The contribution such unglamorous work made to the war effort should not be underestimated, and such patrolling played a crucial part in Britain's ultimate victory. In February 1940, application and endurance secured their just reward when another No.224 Squadron Hudson located the German prison ship the *Altmark* which allowed for its interception by HMS *Cossack* and the liberation of over 200 British prisoners.

Leuchars remained an active station to the end of the war, concentrating on anti-submarine and anti-shipping strikes. With the contraction of the Air Force in peacetime, life at Leuchars returned to a more gentle pace, hosting a school for general reconnaissance and the St Andrews University Air Squadron complete with Tiger Moths. In May 1950 Leuchars entered the jet age as it passed from Coastal to Fighter Command and Gloster Meteors of No.222 Squadron made the station their new home. In time, the first generation of jet aircraft such as the Meteor and Vampire have given way to the Gloster Javelin, the Hawker Hunter, the EE Lightning, the Phantom and the Tornado.

In 1954 the fixed-wing aircraft had been joined by a flight of Sycamore helicopters for Search and Rescue duties, a role subsequently undertaken by the Whirlwind and then the Wessex. From the beginning, the flight proved a valuable adjunct to civilian mountain and maritime rescue services.

As the Cold War reached its frostiest depths in the 1960s the development of long-range aircraft allowed the Soviets regular incursion into British airspace. Initially this was countered by the use of Lightning and, from 1969, Phantom aircraft. Again Leuchars' position made it ideally suited as a base to ensure the integrity of British airspace. For over two decades Leuchars' aircraft have policed the UK air defence region, demonstrating the ability to intercept unidentified aircraft and thereby providing an effective deterrent. The guardianship of British airspace is currently, at 2010 values, vested in the Tornado F.3 Interceptors of No.111 (Fighter) Squadron.

April 2003 saw the Tornado F.3 Conversion Unit (OCU), No.56 [Reserve] Squadron, operating from RAF Leuchars. In April 2008 No.56 [Reserve] Squadron amalgamated with No.43 (Fighter) Squadron. The newly merged squadron was No.43 (Fighter) Squadron.

In July 2009 the newly merged No.43 (Fighter) Squadron saw its formal disbandment parade and flypast at RAF Leuchars. Its place will be taken by a re-forming No.6 Squadron operating the Eurofighter Typhoon FGR.4 and when that unit is declared operational the station will bid farewell to the ageing but very capable Tornado F.3.

A quartet of No.111 Squadron Tornado F.3s prepare to depart the VC.10 tanker following an in-flight refuelling over the North Sea.

CHAPTER 12

NO.43 SQUADRON

NO.43 SQUADRON is synonymous with Scotland and has spent most of its career and certainly the bulk of its home-based service in Scotland. Re-equipping with the Panavia Tornado F.3 on 23 September 1989, although it received its first aircraft for familiarisation a month earlier, the squadron was to see twenty years of service with the Tornado.

The squadron was formed at Stirling on 15 April 1916, as a unit of the Royal Flying Corps, moving to France in 1917 for the spring offensive.

After wartime service in Europe the squadron disbanded in 1919 but re-formed at RAF Henlow in 1925 with Sopwith Snipes. In 1926 the squadron converted to Gloster Gamecocks, thus

With full burner and cleaning up as it accelerates along RAF Marham's runway on 2 April 1993, ZH554/GJ had been representing the squadron at the Queen's Review of the RAF. The aircraft itself was one of the cancelled order for Oman that the RAF received by default. Today it is one of a handful of aircraft to still be in use with No.111 Squadron.

Apart from a short period in 2003 when with No.56 [R] Squadron, ZE207 spent nearly fifteen years with No.43 Squadron. It joined the unit in 1991 as 'GC' and remained current until sometime in 2002 when it suffered a bird strike. Following repairs with TASF at Leuchars it was re-issued to No.56 [R] Squadron as 'UH' in line with the individual coding programme. During its time with the squadron it gained the 'Fireblirds 2003' motif but was later transferred back to 43 Squadron still coded 'UH'. By June 2004 it had regained its original code. It is seen here on 23 July 1997 as 'Blacksmith 3' on refuelling area 8 over the North Sea.

inspiring the squadron badge and the nickname 'The Fighting Cocks'. The squadron flew Siskins from 1928 and Hawker Furies from 1931.

In 1939 the squadron operated Hawker Hurricanes from RAF Tangmere, covering the Dunkirk retreat and fighting in the Battle of Britain, during which the squadron was credited with sixty 'kills'. Later, operating Spitfires, the squadron joined the Desert Air Force and supported the Sicily landings and the advance through Italy into southern France. In 1949 the squadron, which had disbanded two years previously, again re-formed and entered

the jet age with Gloster Meteors. It came to Leuchars in 1950 and in 1954 became the first squadron to receive the Hawker Hunter.

Her Majesty the Queen presented No.43 (Fighter) Squadron with its colours for the first time in June 1957 at RAF Leuchars, returning once again in May 1988 to present a replacement standard.

During most of the 1960s the squadron was based in Cyprus and Aden, where it disbanded on 14 October 1967. In 1969, the Fighting Cocks returned to RAF Leuchars and began flying the Phantom FG.1 aircraft, operating in the maritime air defence role.

With titles on the fin to mark the RAF's 90th Anniversary, ZG774/GV is seen on 2 June 2009 in the Cader Idris pass whilst operating in low flying area 7 (LFA7), Wales. Tornado F.3s did not often operate in the low level, although there was a requirement to maintain a currency on that type of flying. Upon demise of the squadron ZG774 passed to 111 Squadron with whom it is still current.

The low-level environment is a demanding scenario and a skill that has to be practised to stop it degrading. It is also extremely impressive from a bystander's viewpoint when seeing such fast-moving aircraft cruise past below you. From a photographer's perspective it is also a very demanding scenario and one equally as rewarding. Here ZG774 can be seen approaching the Cader Idris pass from the direction of Bala at around 480 knots.

After operating for almost twenty years with the Phantom, the squadron began re-equipping with the Tornado F.3 aircraft in July 1989 and was declared operational one year later, although the impact of the first Gulf War did not see it, or the station, resume its normal 'Northern Q' state until January 1991. In November 1990 the squadron deployed to Saudi Arabia as the lead RAF Tornado F.3 squadron at Dhahran and was on active service throughout the Gulf War, returning to RAF Leuchars in March 1991.

Between 1993 and 1995 the squadron flew operationally in support of Operation Deny Flight over Bosnia-Herzegovina, and since 1998 squadron crews have been deployed on a rotational basis to Saudi Arabia to mount Offensive Counter Air missions over Iraq in support of Operations Bolton and Resinate. The squadron became the first RAF Tornado F.3 unit to be declared operational with both AMRAAM and JTIDS.

The use of in-flight refuelling has always been a major part of the Tornado F.3 game plan. Although blessed with good range and loiter time, use of AAR was paramount to providing extensive CAP coverage as well as becoming a force extender. Here a pair of No.43 Squadron aircraft, including ZE254/UD, takes on fuel from a No.101 Squadron VC.10K3 ZA149. Without such assets the Tornado F.3 force would have been less effective.

Exercise Flying Fish joint 43/111 Squadron exercise patch.

In April 1997 the RAF deployed two squadrons of fighters to the Royal Malaysian Air Base at Butterworth as part of the five nations IADS Exercise. Codenamed 'Flying Fish', this high-profile exercise was aimed to show China the UK's commitment to the region following the handover of Hong Kong. One of the squadrons to deploy was No. 111 Squadron and with them they brought six Tornado F.3s drawn from the Leuchars wing, including ZE755/ GJ, seen here in the flow-through sun sheds at Butterworth. No.43 Squadron relieved its sister squadron mid-way through the exercise and was responsible for their return to the UK.

In February 2003, the Fighting Cocks were part of the RAF Leuchars Wing deployment to Prince Sultan Air Base in Saudi Arabia, from where they launched Offensive Counter Air missions to dominate the Iraqi airspace in support of Operation Telic, the United Nations mission in Iraq. The squadron returned to RAF Leuchars with the disbandment of the RAF presence in Saudi Arabia at the end of April 2003.

The squadron continued to provide UK air defence in the form of twenty-four-hour Quick Reaction Alert, both at RAF Leuchars in Scotland and at RAF Mount Pleasant in the Falkland Islands.

In 2005, the squadron were honoured to receive the 'Freedom of the City of Stirling', the birthplace of 43 Squadron. This prestigious award marks the first time that any RAF squadron has been awarded the freedom of any city and it cemented 43 Squadron's historic ties with the city of its foundation.

1996 saw the squadron deploy to Gwalior air base, India, for the first RAF/Indian Air Force series of Indradhanush exercises; the Indians visited the UK the following year.

As part of the Tornado F.3 force drawdown, No.43 (Fighter) Squadron and No.56 [Reserve] Squadron, the Operational Conversion Unit (OCU), merged on 25 April 2008 under 'Project Waterfront'.

This new merged squadron, named No.43 (Fighter) Squadron, was significantly bigger than the normal unit and extended its current front-line role to include the OCU's task of training *ab initio* pilots and weapon systems officers. The new squadron was also to be responsible for other advanced training including, amongst others, the Qualified Weapons Instructor (QWI) course.

The new squadron increased its establishment to twenty-six aircraft, thirty pairs of permanent aircrew and about 260 engineering personnel. This increase in size necessitated a move from the HAS accommodation to the 'waterfront' line on the north-west of the airfield. The squadron disbanded on 13 July 2009.

UNIT MARKINGS

The black gamecock naturally adorned the aircraft of 'The Fighting Cocks', the insignia being placed in the middle of the fin. Codes (in the 'Gx' range) were in white, edged in black and are placed on the upper fin. Black and white chequered nose-bars are applied either side of the nose roundel.

By 1988 the nose-bars began disappearing and the cockerel insignia was of a much reduced size and repositioned higher on the fin. The fin code was also reduced in size and began being repositioned on the trailing edge of the fin tip, although still in white. Later, though, the nose-bars were to be re-applied and the fin gained a chequered band across the top whilst the cockerel, although still smaller than originally applied, was placed more centrally. The white code letters were once again positioned immediately below the fin band.

Sporting No.43 (F) Squadron's 90th anniversary scheme, ZG757 is seen off Newcastle on 30 April 2007 whilst operating as part of a four-ship mission from RAF Leuchars. The aircraft is in clean configuration and fitted with an inert ASRAAM training round.

CHAPTER 13

NO.111 SQUADRON

NO.111 SQUADRON was the second of the RAF Leuchars-based squadrons to re-equip with the Panavia Tornado F.3. The squadron flew its last operational Phantom FG.1 sortie on 31 October 1989 some four months after No.43 Squadron. After this 'Northern Q' passed temporarily into the hands on the Leeming Wing.

The 'new' No.111 (designate) Squadron flew its first Tornado F.3 sortie in May 1990 and was declared operational on 1 January 1991. As with the other six Tornado F.3 squadrons, 111 took its turn in overseas peacekeeping duties undertaking deployments to Gioia del Colle as part of the UNIPROFOR Deny Flight operation

No.111 Squadron are no strangers to colourful markings. They had the famous 'Black Arrows' aerobatic display team with Hawker Hunters whilst their Lightning F.3s also received a similar scheme to that on ZG753/HH. The Phantom era produced a number of special schemes also, with XV574/Z being perhaps the nicest and broadly similar to this that was produced for 2005.

A tight formation post-refuelling off the tanker comprising of ZE251/UF, Export 2, with ZE159/UV in No.111 Squadron special marks outboard as 'Scimitar 2', whilst ZE936/XF, 'Scimitar 1', lurks in the corner. Captured over the North Sea on 5 September 2003, the special marked jet was retired shortly after this shot was taken.

during which time the squadron flew the mission's 5,000th Operation Grapple (the UK operational code-name) sortie since it first began on 19 April 1993.

In 1997 it was chosen to spearhead the RAF's contribution to Exercise Flying Fish at Butterworth Air Base, Malaysia. The exercise was part of the IADS series but coincided with the handover of Hong Kong back to communist China.

The squadron also undertook the first ever deployment to Lithuania when it took over the NATO QRA detachment to protect the Baltic area. Four aircraft were involved in the detachment

to Siauliai on 4 October 1997, known colloquially as Operation Solstice.

In what is most probably the final overseas deployment by the Tornado F.3, No.111 Squadron deployed six aircraft, ZE961/HB, ZE168/HH, ZE164/HO, ZE342/HP, ZH554/HX and ZE163/HY to RAF Gibraltar on 21 June 2010 for Exercise Southern Flame. Lasting for two weeks, the exercise involved two waves of take-offs and landings each working day. The take-offs were at 09.30 and 13.30 with each sortie lasting between 60 and 90 minutes.

The last of the No.111 Squadron special schemes to be applied to the Tornado F.3 was that of ZE734/JU which it received in May 2007, after the jet had been transferred from No.43 Squadron. It was captured here low level in LFA17 by Brian Hodgeson.

The days of NATO exchange visits or 'Ample Train' cross-servicing exercises are long gone, leaving most front-line fighter squadrons with limited opportunities to train against differing adversaries. Here, however, we have a shot by Brian Boyle of a pair of Canadian Forces CF.188 Hornets from 409 Squadron/CF on just such an exercise with 111 Squadron at RAF Leuchars back in 1991. Sadly the Canadians no longer base any aircraft in Europe, so such opportunities cannot be repeated.

Low-level photography offers those who have to keep their feet on the ground some really dynamic opportunities, as depicted here as Tornado F.3 ZH556/HT provides a plan view with the Snowdonia Range as a backdrop as it manoeuvres in the demanding environment during a sortie on 18 February 2008.

Caught over the Cairngorms during a Joint Warrior Exercise on 22 April 2008, the difference in colour schemes between ZE983/WY, Export 3, and ZE162/HM, Export 4, is clearly demonstrated. The former still retains the older individual airframe coding devised in 2002 whilst the latter has reverted to the preferred individual squadron codes. ZE983 was assigned the code 'HL' but this was not applied until over a year later.

However, the tension between the Spanish and the British security forces stretched over another few degrees, when Spain openly refused to allow the Royal Air Force to use the airspace near Gibraltar for military exercise purposes.

The southern area of the Alboran training zone lies in the Western Mediterranean, which is under the control of Moroccan authorities, whereas the northern region falls under the Spanish zone. While Spain has clearly denied the use of its airspace, Rabat, on the other hand, granted access to the squadron for using the Moroccan airspace.

The spokesman informed that initially an application was submitted to the Spanish for the grant of their airspace. Whilst the Spanish refused British 'requests', the Moroccans gave authority to carry on with our training sessions in the southern half. Therefore the venerable Tornado F.3 is shrouded in controversy to the bitter end!

Formed originally at Deir al-Balah, Palestine, on 1 August 1917 as the first dedicated fighter squadron in the region, its two main tasks were to restrict enemy reconnaissance flights and counter the increasing German fighter threat over the Suez. The squadron flew a variety of types available including Bristol Scouts, Monoplanes and Fighters, DH.2s and SE.5s until standardising on the latter type in 1918. As the tide of the war turned, the unit started ground-attack patrols and such was the pilot's skill that the squadron was able to turn the Turkish retreat into a rout. 'Treble One' withdrew to Egypt after the end of the war and was renumbered No.14 Squadron in February 1920. 1 October 1923 saw No.111 Squadron re-form, this time at RAF Duxford, but again with a variety of types namely Grebes, Snipes and Siskins, the latter eventually equipping the whole squadron, until the arrival of Bristol Bulldogs in 1931.

Five years later, No.111 Squadron received Gloster Gladiators, and in January 1938 the unit had the distinction of becoming the first Hawker Hurricane squadron. The squadron flew as part of both Nos 11 and 12 Groups during the Battle of Britain and replaced its Hurricanes with Spitfires in April 1942. In November the unit moved to Gibraltar in preparation for Operation Torch – the invasion of North Africa – where it supported the 1st Army through Algeria and Tunisia before moving to Malta in June 1943 to cover the invasion of Sicily. With the Allies advancing through Italy, No.111 moved with them, remaining there until after the cessation of hostilities when it moved to Austria. It was disbanded in May 1947 and did not rejoin the RAF's order of battle until December 1953 when it was re-formed with Gloster Meteors at RAF North Weald.

In 1955 the first Hawker Hunters had arrived, and two years later No.111 Squadron was nominated as the official RAF aerobatic team. At first the team, known as the 'Black Arrows', flew five and then nine aircraft until, at the 1958 Farnborough airshow, the squadron, aided by No.56 Squadron, entered the record books when it successfully looped twenty-two aircraft! In 1961, the unit converted to Lightning F.1s, with successive marks staying until 1974 when Phantom FGR.2s arrived. Following a move from Coningsby to RAF Leuchars, the squadron re-equipped with ex-Royal Navy Phantom FG.1s and these survived until the early 1990s when Tornado F.3s became the squadron mount. The squadron became the final front-line user of the Tornado F.3 and was scheduled to disband on or by 1 April 2011.

UNIT MARKINGS

'Treble One's' ornate insignia, in heraldic parlance 'in front of two swords in saltire, a cross potent quadrat, charged with three seaxes fesswise in pale', is surmounted upon a black disc which itself is placed upon a horizontal black band edged in gold atop the fin. The code letters (in the 'Hx' range) are in white and are placed in the middle of the fin. The nose roundel was surmounted on a black lightning flash, edged in gold, which emanates from abeam the intakes.

In 1999 the first aircraft appeared wearing very much toned down unit insignia. ZE158 'Z' received a dark grey fin band with the squadron insignia superimposed in the centre and a light grey code on the trailing edge. Although most of the squadron's aircraft were so treated, the exception being ZE338 that somehow escaped, the scheme was relatively short-lived with the re-adoption of a black fin stripe with a yellow lightning bolt superimposed being introduced following the next change of command. The squadron insignia also reappeared positioned centrally on the fin.

CHAPTER 14

NO.56 SQUADRON

The RAF has a glorious history and heritage that due to the dwindling amount of squadrons it is finding hard to preserve. No.56 [R] Squadron is one of the most illustrious, as can be seen by the campaigns inscribed on this Tornado F.3 fin. The squadron at the demise of the Phantom FGR.2 took on the mantle of Tornado F.3 operational conversion from 229 OCU on 1 July 1992, a role it continued to perform for the next sixteen years until it was disbanded at Leuchars on 4 April 2008. In that time it contributed crews to a number of major conflicts, although it will probably never get the recognition it perhaps deserves.

NO.56 SQUADRON relocated from RAF Coningsby on 27 March 2003, taking with it some seventeen aircraft in five formations:

ZE160 'TX', ZE934 'TA', ZE967 'UT'; ZG770 'WK', ZE908 'TB', ZE941 'KT', ZE343 'TI', ZE207 'UI'; ZE966 'VT', ZE889 'XI', XG796 'WC', ZE735 'TG', ZE256 'TP', ZE250 'TR'; ZH556 'PT', ZE812 'XR'; ZE888 'TC'.

The squadron continued to operate in the Operational Conversion role until the drawdown of the Tornado F.3 fleet had reduced significantly. The squadron disbanded on 22 April 2008, passing its role onto No.43 [F] Squadron which at that time became dual hatted.

As well as passing on its OCU mantle, along with it went most of its aircraft and many of its instructors. One female pilot was seen to be wearing a helmet cover inscribed 'I would rather be a Phoenix than a Cock'!

In its sixteen years of Tornado F.3 operation, it has only been the final five that were spent at RAF Leuchars. Schemes over the years changed little, save for the one-off specials when supplying the RAF Display aircraft, although in recent years these have been somewhat less audacious with perhaps one exception. The characteristic red and white chequerboard has, however, been retained faithfully, either on the fin or as nose-bars, as has the famous 'Phoenix rising from the flames' emblem. ZE207/UH depicted here wears the 2003 display mount colour scheme. When this shot was taken on 10 March 2003 the jet had returned to No.43 (F) Squadron and was being flown as 'Gamecock 1' on the day in question.

Most wings tended to operate a pool system with their fleet of aircraft and this often led to difficulties in identifying which was on whose strength. Here seen in refuelling area 5 on 7 March 2008 as 'Gamecock Formation' are ZE786/TG in No.56 [R] Squadron markings together with ZG757 and ZG798/GQ both wearing No.43 (F) Squadron marks.

Probably the most audacious of all colour schemes which have adorned the Tornado F.3 must be this applied to ZE735 to mark the squadron's 90th anniversary in 2006. Being a twin-sticked aircraft it has spent most of its life within the structure of the OCU although its initial formative years were spent with Nos 5 and then 25 Squadrons. It arrived on the OCU in November 1989, remaining on effective strength until retired in November 2008. It was captured here low one evening over Thirlmere Lake in LFA17 on 9 August 2007.

CHAPTER 15

RAF STANLEY

THE RAF PROVIDES key elements of the forces that Headquarters British Forces South Atlantic Islands use to ensure the security of the Falklands, the South Sandwich Islands and South Georgia. Not only through the air-bridge from Brize Norton to Ascension and onwards to the Falkland Islands, but also through deterrence patrols across the immense area between the islands. The RAF also provides Search and Rescue (SAR) support to the islands and across the fisheries conservation zone, whilst a Hercules can be switched from assisting the Falkland Islands Government with fisheries patrolling to providing air transport and parachute supply drops, or medical evacuation. A VC.10K tanker provides air-to-air refuelling for the flight of Eurofighter Typhoon FGR.4 Air Defence fighters that operate from Mount Pleasant Airfield to watch over the islands and guard them from the air. RAF personnel also support and direct in a wide range of roles on the ground. From fighter controllers to the Explosive Ordinance Disposal team who monitor and where necessary dispose of landmines left over from the conflict.

1435 FLIGHT

Following the recapture of the Falkland Islands it was decided to maintain a permanent detachment of air defence fighters in the region to meet the islands' air defence needs.

Initially this was served by a detachment of BAE Systems Harrier GR.3s assigned to 1453 Flight, but on 17 October 1982 these were augmented by nine Phantom FGR.2s drawn from No.29 Squadron, although the detachment eventually reduced in number and was re-numberplated as No.23 Squadron, with crews rotating from all UK-based air defence squadrons.

No.23 Squadron became No.1435 Flight on 1 November 1988 when No.23 Squadron re-equipped with the Tornado F.3 at RAF Leeming. By this time the detachment had been reduced to just four aeroplanes and akin to the flight's history during the siege of Malta the aircraft were named *Faith*, *Hope*, *Charity* and *Desperation*.

The flight re-equipped with the Tornado F.3 in July 1992 with the initial four aircraft, ZE209, ZE790, ZE758 and ZE812, departing RAF Coningsby on 6 July 1992. Over the next seventeen years the flight has maintained an establishment of four aircraft and until September 1999 the maintenance swap over was conducted with a long transatlantic flight. In January 2000 an experiment of shipping the jets to and from the Falklands by Antonov An-124 was undertaken when ZE729, marked 'Airfix Kit 1' and ZE982 ('Airfix Kit 2') were flown out from RAF Coningsby. However, the next swap over in April 2000 was undertaken using the more conventional method.

The introduction of the Boeing C-17A Globemaster III into the RAF inventory with No.99 Squadron gave a rethink to the deployment methods and on 27 November 2001 ZG753 was shipped to the Falklands; the C-17A returning with ZG795 on December 2. This proved successful and the method of changing aeroplanes in the South Atlantic has continued since although where C-17 availability has been limited they have reverted to the Antonov An-124.

The Tornado F.3 detachment came to an end in October 2009 when 1435 Flight became a Typhoon FGR.4 detachment, with the initial four aircraft being flown to the Falklands. The redundant Tornado F.3s, however, were shipped back to the UK to be returned to produce and scrapped.

In the seventeen years that the Tornado F.3 has policed the Falkland waters somewhere in the region of twenty-nine different airframes have been on the strength of 1435 Flight. The individual aircraft have remained in theatre from as little as a few months

ZG776, depicted here, undertook four rotations to the Falkland Islands and it was during the third of these in 2001 that new markings were adopted, severing the connection to No.23 Squadron. The aircraft was captured upon its return to the UK when it was operating with No.111 Squadron. In this shot it was one of a pair, 'Scimitar 1 & 2', on 19 February 2004.

The Tornado F.3 first took over the role of Falkland Islands policeman on 6 July 1992, a duty it performed relentlessly until relieved by the Typhoon FGR.4 in 2009. In that time some twenty-nine different airframes have taken the long journey south, some on more than one occasion. Crews rotated for short periods so as to preserve their operational capability at home, as the limited training opportunities offered in the South Atlantic would have allowed a number of fundamentals to degrade. In this shot we have a pair of No.1435 Flight aircraft, ZG799/D and ZG751/C, with the markings showing deference to its Maltese history, No.23 Squadron from whom it was born in this life and the Falkland Islands crest.

to in some cases over two years, such is the robust nature of the Panavia aeroplane. Whether the Typhoon will weather the South Atlantic conditions equally as well, only time will tell.

UNIT MARKING

In deference to No.23 Squadron the aircraft carried the squadron's blue and red nose-bars either side of the Falkland Islands crest of a white ram on a blue shield. On the tail a large red Maltese Cross was centrally positioned with the aircraft's individual code letter in red towards the bottom of the leading edge of the fin just above the aircraft serial.

In 2004 these changed to a simple red and white stripe across the top of the fin with a Maltese Cross superimposed in the centre.

CHAPTER 16

DESERT STORM – OPERATION GRANBY

THE INVASION OF KUWAIT

THE UK RESPONDS

IT WAS IN the early hours of 2 August 1990 that elements of the Iraqi Republican Guard spearheaded the invasion of Kuwait. Following days of Iraqi 'sabre-rattling', the Kuwait militia offered little resistance to the invaders and the country was more or less under Iraqi control within 24 hours. The Emir of Kuwait, Sheikh Jaber al Ahned al Sabah, was evacuated to neighbouring Saudi Arabia as were a number of Kuwaitis including some 7,000 military personnel. An emergency session of the United Nations Security Council was convened and passed UN Resolution 660, which condemned Iraq for its actions and called for the unconditional withdrawal of Iraqi forces from Kuwait.

It soon became clear that, given the minimal effort made in the taking of Kuwait, Iraqi president Saddam Hussein may now direct his forces to continue south into Saudi Arabia and claim as much of the Saudi oilfields as possible. King Fahd of Saudi Arabia, all too aware of this possibility and the world-wide repercussions this would cause, invited foreign governments to send armed forces to his country to safeguard it from attack. US President George Bush ordered the start of Operation Desert Shield, a massive air and sea-lift of forces to the Gulf region, starting with the transfer of the F-15C Eagles of the USAF's 1st Tactical Fighter King from Langley AFB, VA as well as the substantial force of the US Army's 82nd Airborne Division. These units were directly assigned to the US Central Command (CENTCOM), headed by its Commander-in-Chief, General Norman H. Schwarzkopf, who was to become Supreme Allied Commander for the international forces in the Gulf region.

For many years, Saudi Arabia has been the United Kingdom's closest ally in the Middle East and King Fahd's request for assistance was soon met. Operation Granby was instigated, the name itself having no significance as it was simply the next in the series of computer-generated codewords normally used for UK military operations. HM Government announced on 9 August 1990 that a squadron of Tornado F.3s would deploy to Saudi Arabia and twelve aircraft flew direct from Akrotiri to King Abdul Aziz AB, Dhahran, two days later, these being drawn from No.5 Squadron (which arrived in Cyprus for its annual armament practice camp commencing 7 August 1990) and No.29 Squadron (which was

The first Gulf War, or Operation Granby as it was known in RAF circles, saw the Tornado F.3 as the first UK assets into theatre following Iraq's annexing of Kuwait. Although at the time still hampered by many less than desirable teething troubles, a programme of upgrades meant a number of these were addressed by monies supplied under a 'UOR', Urgent Operational Requirement. This at least gave the crews a workable jet, although many more issues remained. Here over the desert is ZE162/DM, one of the first stage 1+ aircraft to be deployed under the command of Wing Commander David Hamilton. The picture was taken by Robert Hoskins from 'his' RC-135V 'Sigint' aircraft.

due to depart back to the UK following APC on 8 August 1990), both of which were normally stationed at RAF Coningsby. Wing Commander Euan Black, Officer Commanding No.5 Squadron, headed the mixed unit which became known as No.5 (Composite) Squadron. Aircraft deployed were as follows:

ZE289/BA, ZE338/BB, ZE258/BE, ZE254/BG, ZE255/BH, ZE205/BS: all No.29 Sqn.

ZE762/CA, ZE758/CB, ZE163/CF, ZE732/CH, ZE734/CJ, ZE736/CK: all No.5 Sqn.

The unit flew its first combat air patrol (CAP) on 12 August 1990, a further ten crews arrived via Hercules later in the day, and with the ground crew the detachment totalled some 200 personnel.

The balance of aircraft and crews from both units remained at Akrotiri in reserve, as well as providing stand-by air defence cover for Cyprus should the crisis worsen. The senior UK officer in the Gulf from 9 August 1990 was Group Captain Rick Peacock-Edwards, then Station Commander RAF Leeming.

With a large number of RAF assets in or on their way to the region, and following the Royal Navy's command responsibility for the liberation of the Falkland Islands in 1982 (under Operation Corporate), it was the RAF which had the distinction of heading Operation Granby with the appointed Joint Commander-in-Chief being Air Chief Marshal Sir Patrick Hine, then Air Officer Commander-in-Chief Strike Command.

No sooner had these aircraft arrived at Dhahran when it was decided to send the much improved Stage 1+ Tornado F.3s to the region; these aircraft carried the Foxhunter radar upgraded to AA standard, enhanced cockpit controls (i.e. giving the F.3 a hands on throttle-and-stick – 'HOTAS' – operation), surface wave absorbent material (SWAM) painted on all leading edges plus engine intake areas in an effort to reduce the F.3's relatively large radar cross section, uprated RB.199 Mk104 engines, provision for AIM-9M Sidewinder missiles (replacing the AIM-9L normally carried), Have Quick secure communications plus two Tracer ALE-40(V) flare dispensers fitted to the bottom rear fuselage (these were swapped for Vinten VICON 78 series 210 dispensers before the start of Desert Storm, however) and Philips MATRA Phimat chaff dispensers carried on the wing 'shoulder' pylons.

The first three aircraft with this so-called 'war fit' (ZE961/GA, ZE942/GH and ZE936/GK, all from 43 Sqn) arrived at RAF Leeming from RAF Leuchars on 11 August 1990 (namely the same day as their less-capable sisters arrived in Saudi Arabia) in readiness for deployment. During the following days of a remarkably hot August and early September, a large number of F.3s arrived to be readied for transfer to the Gulf region as follows (in arrival date order):

14 August	ZE962/GB, ZE203/GD, ZE887/GE, ZE210/GL – all ex-43 Sqn;
15 August	ZE206/- (ex-'GG'/43 Sqn), ZE934/- ex-111 Sqn/ no marks, ZE965/- (ex-'HA'/111 Sqn), ZE941/CI ex-5 Sqn;
16 August	ZE908/CT ex-5 Sqn;
19 August	ZE162/AW ex-229 OCU/65 Sqn, ZE969/HD ex-111 Sqn;
20 August	ZE968/HE and ZE164/HH both ex-111 Sqn;
21 August	ZE907/- ex-229 OCU/65 Sqn special marks;
22 August	ZE964/- ex-43 Sqn/no marks, ZE966/GF and ZE161/GI both ex-43 Sqn;
23 August	ZE888/- ex-111 Sqn/no marks, ZE204/GJ ex-43 Sqn;
26 August	ZE963 (ex 'GC'/43 Sqn) had arrived by this date;
28 August	ZE982/- ex-production, BAe Warton;
2 August	ZE967/- ex-43 Sqn/no marks had arrived by this date;
3 August	ZE200/AV ex-229 OCU/65 Sqn.

Following each F.3's release to service by the Aircraft Servicing Flight (ASF), codes in the 'DA' to 'DZ' range were applied as the unit to deploy was to be No.XI (C) Squadron under the command of Wing Commander David Hamilton, OC No.11 Squadron at RAF Leeming, with crews also coming from co-resident 23 and 25 Squadrons.

Commencing 29 August 1990, the first of an eventual unit strength of eighteen of these aircraft were sent to the theatre. The unit was nicknamed the 'Desert Eagles' (after 11 Squadron's usual nickname), and a small number of the F.3s received motifs to this effect atop their fins based on the RAF eagle insignia.

Six aircraft from the original deployment of 5/29 Squadron F.3s left Saudi Arabia on 1 September 1990. Before his departure, Wing Commander Euan Black found time to lead a 'Vic' formation of three Tornado F.3s (lead ZE736/CK, accompanied by ZE762/CA, also in

5 Squadron marks, plus Stage 1+ example ZE961/DH) over Dhahran on 15 September 1990; the same day as 168 RAF aircraft overflew central London to mark the 50th anniversary of the Battle of Britain. Black himself flew one of a further five F.3s which departed Dhahran on 17 September 1990, with one example (ZE758/CB, which had become unserviceable) eventually landing back at RAF Coningsby on 27 September 1990. The RAF detachment commander switched from Group Captain Peacock-Edwards to Group Captain John Rooum on 3 October 1990.

PREPARATION FOR WAR

As the initial build-up of international forces climaxed during October 1990, all of which were in effect a deterrent force to stop further Iraqi aggression in the Arabian Peninsula, war-planners from each of the major coalition forces provided countless studies as to how Kuwait could be liberated should all diplomatic processes fail. President George Bush announced on 8 November 1990 that the US military force gathered in the Gulf would be doubled to around 250,000 personnel, thus starting the Allies' move from a defensive to an offensive stance. HM Government announced that the UK would send an additional 20,000 troops to the region; this included a further squadron of Tornado GR.1s plus the 4th Armoured Brigade, which combined with the 'Desert Rats' to form the 1st (British) Armoured Division in theatre. Seven days later, the UN Security Council passed UN Resolution 678, authorising the Allies to use all means necessary to remove Iraqi forces from Kuwait had it not done so by a deadline of 15 January 1991.

Air Vice Marshal William 'Bill' Wratten (at the time AOC No.11 Group, and later Air Chief Marshal Sir William Wratten as AOC-in-C Strike Command) took over as Air Commander and Deputy Commander BFME from 'Sandy' Wilson on 17 November 1990. Also during the month, Air Commodore Ian MacFadyen took post as de la Billiere's Chief of Staff.

The deadline for the unconditional withdrawal of Iraqi forces from Kuwait passed on 15 January 1991 with no movement by Saddam Hussein's forces. The bulk of flying training by the Allied air forces had ceased on 13 January 1991, permitting an adjustment in crew shift patterns in preparation for active service, as well as giving maintenance personnel a period in which to bring their fleets up to full combat readiness.

TORNADO AIR DEFENCE

As covered earlier, the enhanced air defence forces in place in Saudi Arabia from mid-August 1990 formed a crucial deterrent to the spread of Saddam Hussein's aggression in the Arabian Peninsula. The Tornado F.3s based at Dhahran routinely flew their CAPs in an area just south of the Iraq and Kuwait borders with Saudi Arabia, with these missions being maintained around the clock. Perhaps the biggest surprise of the war to the Allies was the almost non-existent response from the Iraqi Air Force, which could boast aircraft such as the MiG-29 'Fulcrum' in its inventory. The nearest action seen by the F.3 detachment occurred on 18 January 1991, when two aircraft (one of which had the CO, Wing Commander Andy Moir, aboard) entered occupied Kuwaiti airspace following reports that a flight of USAF A-10A Thunderbolt II's were being engaged by Iraqi fighters, thought to be Dassault

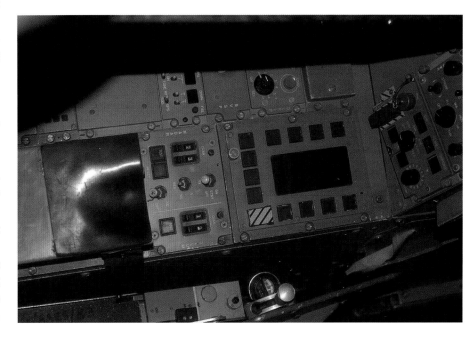

One of the many upgrades initiated through the UOR was the retrofitting of the jets deployed with secure communications, including the provision of the 'Have Quick' radio seen in this shot.

Mirage F.ls. The two F.3s 'cleaned' (i.e. blowing-off their external fuel tanks) and headed at high speed towards the retreating Thunderbolt II's and soon obtained a radar lock-on to the Iraqi aircraft, which promptly disengaged and headed northbound. A handful of similar instances also took place in the early days of the war, although CAPs were being flown above Kuwait City by 21 January 1991, such was the air supremacy of the Allied forces.

By the end of hostilities on 28 February 1991, the eighteen F.3 aircraft had flown some 2,500 sorties during their deployment, of which the detachment flew 360 combat sorties; it ceased operations on 8 March 1991, with all aircraft and equipment leaving Dhahran seven days later.

All aircraft retained their barley grey air superiority camouflage. Although only white code letters were usually applied to the centre of the fin, some aircraft received 'Desert Eagles' insignia (including ZE968/DJ). These were removed by the time of OC No.43 Squadron taking over the detachment during December 1990, when the unit also switched to single-letter codes, and these are listed subsequently to those in the 'DA' to 'DZ' range:

ZE203/DA	*Airspare 29.8.90, flew Leeming–Akrotiri–Dhahran 22/23.9.90. See ZE203/A later.*
ZE204/DB	*Leeming–Akrotiri–Dhahran 16/17.9.90; see ZE204/B later.*
ZE206/DC	*Leeming–Akrotiri–Dhahran 29/30.8.90; see ZE206/C later.*
ZE210/DD	*Leeming–Akrotiri–Dhahran 29/30.8.90; returned to Leuchars 20.11.90 (see ZE210/G).*
ZE887/DE	*Reserve a/c; see ZE887/E later.*
ZE936/DF	Leeming–Akrotiri–Dhahran 29/30.8.90; see ZE936/F later.
ZE942/DO	Leeming–Akrotiri–Dhahran 16/17.9.90; returned to Leuchars 21.11.90.
ZE961/DH	Leeming–Akrotiri–Dhahran 29/30.8.90; see ZE962/I later.
ZE968/DJ	Leeming–Akrotiri–Dhahran 29/30.8.90; see ZE968/J later.
ZE907/DK	Leeming–Akrotiri–Dhahran 22/23.9.90; see ZE907/K later.
ZE969/DL	Leeming–Akrotiri–Dhahran 16/17.9.90; see ZE969/L later.
ZE162/DM	Leeming–Akrotiri–Dhahran 16/17.9.90; returned to Leeming 12.1.91.
ZE159/DO	Leeming–Akrotiri–Dhahran 22/23.9.90; see ZE159/O later.
ZE982/DP	Leeming–Akrotiri–Dhahran 16/17.9.90; see ZE982/P later.
ZE164/DQ	Reserve a/c; see ZE164/G later.
ZE967/DR	Reserve a/c; never deployed.
ZE964/DS	Airspare 22.9.90, reserve a/c and never deployed.
ZE888/DT	Leeming–Akrotiri–Dhahran 16/17.9.90; see ZE888/T later.
ZE165/DU	Airspare 16.9.90, flew Leeming–Akrotiri–Dhahran 22/23.9.90; see ZE165/U later.
ZE934/DV	Airspare 29.8.90, reserve a/c; See ZE934/Q later.
ZE941/DW	Leeming–Akrotiri–Dhahran 22/23.9.90; returned to Leuchars 19.11.90.
ZE963/DX	Airspare 16.9.90, flew Leeming–Akrotiri–Dhahran 22/23.9.90; Returned to Leuchars 22.11.90.
ZE965/DY	Airspare 22.9.90, reserve a/c and never deployed.
ZE200/DZ	Reserve a/c; see ZE200/L later.
ZE966/DZ	Reserve a/c; see ZE966/Y later.
ZE203/A	Ex-'DA'; returned to Coningsby 14.3.91.
ZE763/A	Leeming–Dhahran during 2.91; noted in full 29 Sqn markings on 25.2.91, coded 'BA'; Returned to Coningsby 13.3.91.
ZE204/B	Ex-'DB'; returned to Coningsby 13.3.91.
ZE206/C	Ex-'DC'; returned to UK middle of 3.91.
ZE158/D	Leuchars–Dhahran 18.11.90. Returned to UK during 2.91.
ZE201/E	Leeming–Dhahran during 2.91; Dhahran–Decimomannu–Leuchars 12/13.3.91.
ZE887/E	Leuchars–Dhahran 11.1.91 (uncoded at that time, although 'E' code conflicted with ZE201/E above and was soon removed); Returned to Coningsby 13.3.91.
ZE936/P	Ex-'DF'; returned to Leeming 12.1.91.
ZE164/G	Leuchars–Dhahran 18.11.90 (uncoded at that time); returned to UK mid-3.91.
ZE210/O	Leeming–Dhahran during 2.91; Dhahran–Decimomannu–Leuchars 12/13.3.91.
ZE961/H	Ex-'DH'; returned to Coningsby 13.3.91.

ZE764/I	Leeming–Dhahran 2/3.91 (f/n 11.3.91); Dhahran–Decimomannu–Leuchars 12/13.3.91.
ZE962/I	Ex-'DI'; returned to Leeming 12.1.91.
ZE968/J	Ex-'DJ'; returned to UK mid-3.91 (Coningsby on 13.3.917).
ZE737/K	Leeming–Dhahran during 2.91; Dhahran–Decimomannu–Leuchars 12/13.3.91.
ZE907/K	Ex-'DK'; returned to Leeming during 2.91 although was reported unmarked/uncoded at Dhahran on 6.3.91.
ZE200/L	Leuchars–Dhahran 18.11.90 (uncoded at that time); returned to UK by end 3.91.
ZE969/L	Ex-'DL'; returned to Coningsby 14.3.91.
ZE159/O	Ex-'DO'; returned to Leeming 12.2.91.
ZE982/P	Ex-'DP'; returned to Leeming 12.2.91.
ZE934/Q	UK (Leeming?)–Dhahran 11.1.91 (uncoded); returned to Leeming by 23.2.91.
ZE161/R	Leeming–Dhahran 11.1.91 (uncoded at that time); returned to UK during 3.91.
ZE941/R	Leeming–Dhahran during 2.91; returned to Coningsby 13.3.91.
ZE888/T	Ex-'DT'; returned to Leeming 12.1.91.
ZE165/U	Ex-'DU'; returned to Leeming 12.2.91.
ZE199/W	Leeming–Dhahran during 2.91; Dhahran–Decimomannu–Leuchars 12/13.3.91.
ZE908/X	Leuchars–Dhahran 18.11.90 (uncoded at that time); returned to UK mid-3.91.
ZE966/Y	UK (Leuchars?)–Dhahran during 2.91. Recoded 'GF' and full 43 Sqn marks applied by 11.3.91. Flew Dhahran–Decimomannu–Leuchars 12/13.3.91.
ZE160/Z	Leeming–Dhahran during 2.91; returned to Coningsby 13.3.91.

Deployments to Dhahran (aircraft unknown) commenced on the following: 11.2.91 (three a/c), plus 14.2.91 (three a/c), 20.2.91 (three a/c) and 28.2.91 (four a/c). Three aircraft flew Dhahran–Decimomannu–Leeming on 1/2.3.91; other returning aircraft are listed above. Reproduced courtesy of BAR.

No sooner had the Tornado F.3s returned from duties in the Gulf then they were thrust into the NATO-led operation to police the Balkans. Known collectively as Operation Deny Flight. Once again it was the stage 1+ aircraft that were deployed and as these were more or less all assigned to the Leeming Wing it led to a great deal of shuffling and loan of the aircraft at both Coningsby and Leuchars to keep the home-based squadrons with aircraft with which to operate. Based at Gioia del Colle in Italy, this deployment was to last until February 1996. Seen here at Gioia del Colle is ZE161/FG on 22 August 1995.

CHAPTER 17

DENY FLIGHT – OPERATION GRAPPLE

IN OCTOBER 1992, at the beginning of the Bosnian War, the United Nations Security Council passed Resolution 781. This resolution prohibited unauthorised military flights in Bosnian airspace. Following the resolution, NATO began Operation Sky Monitor, during which NATO forces monitored violations of the no-fly zone, without taking any military action against violators. By April 1993, NATO forces had documented more than 500 violations of the no-fly zone. In response to these 'blatant' violations of Bosnian airspace, and implicitly of Resolution 781, the UN Security Council issued Resolution 816.

While Resolution 781 prohibited only military flights, Resolution 816 prohibited all flights in Bosnian airspace, except for those expressly authorised by the UN Flight Coordination Center in Zagreb.

NATO therefore implemented a no-fly zone over the airspace of beleaguered Bosnia-Herzegovina on 12 April 1993 in an attempt to make the population safe from air attack by Serbian air force aircraft; a situation prompted by the raid by three Antonov An-2 'Colt' aircraft on a Muslim village near the besieged town of Srebrenica on 15 March. Code-named Operation Deny Flight by NATO, a number of countries offered aircraft to enforce the ban including the United States, Holland, Italy and France.

The United Kingdom response was to send six Panavia Tornado F.3 fighters, ZE164/DA, ZE964/DY, ZE20/ED, ZE936/EE, ZE159/EG and ZE961/FD, from No.11 (composite) Squadron at RAF Leeming to Gioia del Colle in Italy on 19 April 1993 along with two VC.10 tankers from RAF Brize Norton to Sigonella. By 3 May Allied fighters had flown 706 operational sorties. A further two Tornado F.3s were deployed a month later on 13 May.

Later in July RAF Jaguars were also deployed to Gioia del Colle which, along with other NATO attack assets, would be used to support Allied peacekeepers on the ground.

An RAF landmark was recorded on 23 July 1994 when the 5,000th Tornado F.3 hour was flown. Flight Lieutenant Gordon MacLeod and Flying Officer Shaun Vickers of No.111 Squadron landed back at Gioia del Colle at 03.00 after a five-hour patrol supporting the UN operation.

Each RAF squadron was to spend a two-month period on rotation at the Italian base. No.11 Squadron were in situ from April to June 1993 followed by No.23 Squadron from June to August, then 25 Squadron, 5 Squadron, 29 Squadron, 43 Squadron and 111 Squadron.

The aircraft were all Tornado F.3 Stage 1+ aircraft drawn from the Leeming Wing. As such there was a considerable amount of swapping and loaning of aircraft back in the UK to fill the shortfall at Leeming.

The operations of Deny Flight spanned more than two years of the Bosnian War and played an important role in the course of that conflict. The no-fly zone operations of Deny Flight proved successful in preventing significant use of air power by any side in

In the event of a hostile contact, the Tornado F.3 would blow the external tanks to hasten the intercept. Here a No.111 Squadron F.3 can be seen in clean configuration at low level.

the conflict. Additionally, the air strikes flown during Deny Flight led to Operation Deliberate Force, a massive NATO bombing campaign in Bosnia that played a key role in ending the war.

This in turn led to conflict between the two organisations, NATO and the UN. Most notably, significant tension arose between the two after UN peacekeepers were taken as hostages in response to NATO bombing.

The no-fly zone was not totally successful in preventing aggression against Bosnia but at least meant that Allied assets were in place and in a position to intercept any such acts. The first serious violation to the no-fly zone came on 28 February 1994, when six Serb J-21 Jastreb jets bombed a Bosnian factory. USAF Lockheed Martin F-16C Fighting Falcons shot down four of the six Serb jets over Banja Luka, in what became known as the Banja Luka incident. This engagement was the first combat engagement in Deny Flight, and its only significant air-to-air combat engagement. Perhaps more importantly, the Banja Luka incident was also the first combat engagement in the history of NATO. Against helicopter action the problem was not easily confronted.

After the adoption of the Dayton Accords, a peace agreement for Bosnia, Deny Flight's mission was no longer necessary. On 15 December 1995, the United Nations Security Council officially terminated the resolutions that had authorised the operation, and on 16 December, the North Atlantic Council agreed to terminate Operation Deny Flight, effective 20 December. On 21 December 1995, NATO held a formal closure ceremony for Deny Flight in Vicenza. Many of the forces assigned to Deny Flight were transferred to Operation Decisive Endeavor, to provide support for new IFOR peacekeepers in Bosnia.

The RAF Tornado F.3s still at Gioia del Colle remained in situ until February 1996 when the eight aircraft, ZE204/DD, ZE969/DI, ZE983/DN, ZE965/DW, ZE961/FD, ZE962/FJ, ZE907/FM and ZE963/FT, returned to RAF Leeming.

Sunset Combat Air Patrol (CAP), 13 January 2005.

CHAPTER 18

2003 IRAQ WAR – OPERATION TELIC

AIR OPERATIONS BY British forces during the second Gulf campaign in 2003 went under the heading of Operation Telic and were to continue for six long years after hostilities finished.

However, in so far as the Panavia Tornado F.3's contribution was concerned, this was to be brief and to the point; tasked in theatre to neutralise the counter-air threat.

In loose echelon this four-ship of aircraft from No.43 Squadron, seen on refuelling area 4 as 'Gamecock 1 to 4' on 10 March 2004, is led by ZE206/UI still sporting the second Gulf conflict nose art, comprising a young lady on port side with inscription 'Tracy Shaw Thing'. The Tornado F.3 played a relatively minor role in the operation to topple Saddam Hussein, being brief and to the point in theatre to neutralise the counter-air threat.

The outbound deployments to the Gulf region commenced during January 2003 with in-theatre operations effectively commencing on 20 March and it is generally accepted that these lasted for twenty-six days, finishing on 14 April after US forces captured Tikrit.

The following Tornado F.3s were deployed to Al Kharj, Saudi Arabia on Operation Resinate South during January 2003: ZE161/UU, ZE162/UR, ZE808/XV, ZE942/XE, ZE961/XD and ZE962/XC. Only two examples of these were to return to the UK prior to the conflict commencing: ZE942/XE departed Al Kharj on 13 February to Akrotiri, arriving at St Athan on 14 February, and 'RRR9578', ZE961/XD, departed Al Kharj on 3 March for the UK, possibly to Leuchars as an unidentified aircraft, 'RRR9503', arrived around this date.

Departures from the UK out to the Gulf commenced on 10 February 2003, with the bulk of the movements taking place two weeks later on 24 February:

10 February	ZE737/YM u/m departed Leuchars as 'RFR9579' to Akrotiri. A second aircraft, 'RFR9578', aborted departure.
11 February	ZE206/UI u/m departed Leuchars as 'RFR9578' to Akrotiri, delayed from the previous day.
15 February	ZE342/(YS) departed from St Athan to Akrotiri as 'RRR9578' as a replacement for ZE942/XE.
24 February	Departures took place from both Leeming and Leuchars and totalled eight aircraft, all at Akrotiri by 25 February.

From Leuchars 'RRR9691-9693' departed which were identified as ZE758/YI and ZE968/XB, although the third example requires confirmation but is believed from the process of elimination to be ZE164/UQ.

From Leeming 'RRR9694-9696' departed, joining up with the three aircraft from Leuchars (for serials, see later).

Some fourteen aircraft took part in Operation Telic with outbound deployments to the Gulf region commencing in January 2003; operations effectively started on 20 March and it is generally accepted that these lasted for twenty-six days, finishing on 14 April after the US captured Tikrit. Many of the aircraft involved received nose art and this was retained until they entered their next major servicing. Seen at Waddington in July 1993 is ZE737/YM unmarked but displaying nose art depicting 'Roger the Dodger'.

ZE161/UU in No.43 Squadron markings carried a cartoon of the Foghorn Leghorn cartoon character with Union Jack feathers and holding a sword through a caricature of Saddam's head with the inscription 'Operation Telic 43'. Photographed at RAF Waddington in July 2003.

A single aircraft departed Leuchars, ZE165/UP 'RFR7443A', which joined up with 'RFR7443B' from Leeming – both aircraft were requesting Nice as a landing point prior to Akrotiri.

The eight aircraft that were in situ at RAF Akrotiri on 25 February were: ZE158/(UW), ZE164/UQ, ZE162/UR, ZE731/YP, ZE758/YI, ZE831/XQ, ZE907/XH and ZE968/XB. All were then repositioned to Al Kharj, Saudi Arabia, by 2 March, with the exception of ZE165/UP that arrived two days later on 4 March.

The fourteen aircraft that look part in Operation Telic were: ZE158/(UW), ZE161/UU, ZE162/UR, ZE164/UQ, ZE165/UP, ZE206/UI, ZE731/YP, ZE737/YM, ZE758/YI, ZE808/XV, ZE831/XQ, ZE907/XH, ZE962/XC and ZE968/XB.

All fourteen aircraft returned to Leuchars during April 2003:

11 April	'RRR9594/95/97' – ZE161/UU, ZEI62/UR, ZE737/YM; 'RRR9596' – ZE831/XQ (returned via a stop at Marham); 'RRR9598-9599' – ZE164/UQ, ZE808/XV.
17 April	'RRR9600-9606' – ZE907/XH, ZE968/XB, ZE731/YP, ZE158/(UW), ZE758/YI, ZE962/XC, ZE206/UI.
18 April	'RRR9607' – ZE165/UP.

A number of the aircraft received special markings and included various artworks with names of RAF war aces together with the number of their aerial victories:

ZE158/-	111 Sqn tail marks; named 'McCudden/57', four Ace playing cards on starboard side of the nose wheel door.
ZE161/UU	43 Sqn tail marks; named 'Lacey/28', four Ace playing cards, artwork on port side comprised Foghorn Leghorn cartoon character with Union Jack feathers and holding a sword through a caricature of Saddam's head with the inscription 'Operation Telic 43'.
ZE162/UR	111 Sqn tail marks; named 'Proctor/54', four Ace playing cards on starboard side, no nose artwork.
ZE164/UQ	111 Sqn tail marks; no name noted and no artwork carried.

ZE165/UP	No details reported.
ZE206/UI	111 Sqn tail marks; named 'Bader/22', four Ace playing cards on starboard side, artwork young lady on port side with inscription 'Tracy Shaw Thing' and further forward that of the 'Soccer AM' logo under the canopy. On the fuselage were the inscriptions 'The Colonel' beneath the pilot's cockpit and for the WSO's position 'Ginger'.
ZE731/YP	111 Sqn tail marks; named 'Bishop/72', four Ace playing cards on starboard side of nose wheel door and nose art on port side 'Desperate Dan' cartoon character with the inscription 'Desperate Dan'.
ZE737/YM	111 Sqn tail marks; named 'Stanford Tuck/28', four Ace playing cards, nose art on port side 'Roger the Dodger' cartoon character with the inscription 'The Dodger'.
ZE758/YI	111 Sqn tail marks; named 'Caldwell/28', four Ace playing cards, nose art on port side comprising a shark and the word 'Tremble' which had tatty edges, looking like bullet holes.
ZE808/XV	111 Sqn tail marks; no name noted and nose art details not recorded.
ZE831/XQ	111 Sqn tail marks; no name or nose art noted.
ZE907/XH	111 Sqn tail marks; no further details recorded.
ZE962/XC	111 Sqn tail marks; named 'Deere/27', four Ace playing cards on starboard side of nose wheel door and nose art on port side comprised Dennis the Menace cartoon character with the inscription 'Dennis the Menace'.
ZE968/XB	111 Sqn tail marks; named 'Collinshaw/60', four Ace playing cards on starboard side of the nose wheel, no artwork.

The last Tornado F.3 returned to RAF Leuchars on 18 April 2003 and the detachment at Al Kharj was withdrawn shortly afterwards.

CHAPTER 19

ROYAL SAUDI AIR FORCE

AL QUWWAT AL JAWWIYA AS SA'UDIYA

The Royal Saudi Air Force was the first, and only, non-Panavia partner to take delivery of Tornados, although they were preceded by Oman in 1984 in ordering the aircraft; an order that was later cancelled. Malaysia had also considered buying the ADV version, but due to financial constraints opted for twenty Hawk 100/200 series fighters instead.

The Saudi Tornado buy comprised of forty-eight IDS and twenty-four ADV aircraft and was part of a much larger package that also covered the supply of Pilatus PC.9, Scottish Aviation Jetstream and BAE Systems Hawk trainers. BAe is understood to have taken twenty-four surplus Lightning F.53/T.55s in part exchange. These were later offered to Austria who ultimately selected the Saab J 35Oe Draken for its air defence and policing role.

Having finally signed the deal under Al Yamamah I in February 1986, the Saudis then requested early delivery of the aircraft. As such, eighteen RAF and two German IDS aircraft were diverted from batch 5 production. In the case of the ADV aircraft, these were diverted from RAF batch 6 orders, as can be seen in chapter 21, 'Aircraft Service Details'.

The first Tornado ADV for the RSAF to fly was 2905; this taking place on 1 December 1988. Initial deliveries began on 20 March 1989 with four aircraft (2901, 2902, 2905 & 2906) departing Warton for Dhahran to equip No.29 Squadron. Deliveries were completed by 20 September 1989 with the squadron being declared combat-ready shortly afterwards.

It was originally thought that the twenty-four aircraft would eventually equip two squadrons, the second being No.34 Squadron, also co-located at Dhahran. This squadron received its first aircraft on 14 November 1989 and had completely re-equipped by mid-1990. However, soon afterwards the aircraft and crews were absorbed into No.29 Squadron and No.34 Squadron converted to the Boeing F-15C Eagle.

No.29 Squadron added their weight to the overall defence shield during Operations Desert Shield and Desert Storm, mainly flying CAPs. The Tornado ADV had a relatively short history and the surviving twenty-one aircraft were all finally withdrawn from service by August 2006.

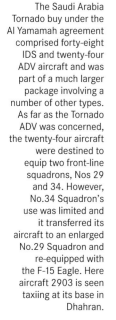

The Saudi Arabia Tornado buy under the Al Yamamah agreement comprised forty-eight IDS and twenty-four ADV aircraft and was part of a much larger package involving a number of other types. As far as the Tornado ADV was concerned, the twenty-four aircraft were destined to equip two front-line squadrons, Nos 29 and 34. However, No.34 Squadron's use was limited and it transferred its aircraft to an enlarged No.29 Squadron and re-equipped with the F-15 Eagle. Here aircraft 2903 is seen taxiing at its base in Dhahran.

CHAPTER 20

THE ITALIAN CONNECTION

DURING NOVEMBER 1993 the Italian Defence Minister met with the UK Defence Secretary Malcolm Rifkind to discuss, amongst other things, the possibility of leasing twenty-four RAF Tornado F.3 fighters as a stop-gap package until the arrival of Eurofighter EF2000.

As a consequence, an agreement was reached to supply two batches of twelve aircraft – the first to equip 12 Gruppo 36 Stormo in June 1995 and the second 21 Gruppo 53 Stormo in 1997 as part of a six-year lease.

Crew training was undertaken by No.56 [R] Squadron at RAF Coningsby and deliveries commenced to Gioia del Colle for 36 Stormo in September 1995 and to Cameri for 53 Stormo in February 1997. The latter were to be short-lived with the unit disbanding in September 1999 before the expiry of the lease and the aircraft being re-assigned to 36 Stormo.

At the end of the lease period the bulk of the aircraft were returned to UK charge although one, MM7210 (ex-ZE836), was retained for display purposes. The remaining twenty-three aircraft were predominantly flown to RAF St Athan for storage, with only relatively few returning to operational RAF charge. The remainder were used for parts reclamation and eventually scrapped.

LEASED AIRCRAFT

RAF serial	AMI serial	AMI code	Delivery Date	Return Date
ZE167	MM7234	5314 to 3624	18.07.97	31.03.04
ZE202	MM55056	3601 to 3620	05.09.95	13.10.04
ZE205	MM55061	5312 to 3620	18.07.97	28.07.04
ZE208	MM55060	5301 to 3630	14.03.97	06.08.04
ZE252	MM7225	5302 to 3604	27.03.97	28.05.03
ZE730	MM7204	3605	04.06.97	25.02.04
ZE760	MM7206	3607	21.11.95	24.03.03
ZE761	MM7203	3602	09.09.95	04.08.03
ZE762	MM7207	3610 to 3627	21.12.95	31.03.04
ZE787	MM7205	3606	13.10.95	07.06.04
ZE792	MM7211	3616	29.09.95	24.10.03
ZE811	MM7208	3611 to 3622	12.03.96	05.12.03
ZE832	MM7202	3612	05.07.95	26.03.03
ZE835	MM7209	3613 to 3625	14-03-96	13.10.04
ZE836	MM7210	3614	21.12.95	Pres Vigna di Valle
ZE837	MM55057	3603	04.10.95	28.01.03
ZE911	MM7226	5321 to 3606	14.02.97	07.06.04
ZG728	MM7229	5306 to 3607	23.04.97	04.12.03
ZG730	MM7230	5307 to 3611	04.06.97	28.07.04
ZG732	MM7227	5305 to 3622	24.04.97	04.08.03
ZG733	MM7228	5303 to 3634	09.04.97	23.08.03
ZG734	MM7231	5311 to 3612	17.07.97	05.06.03
ZG735	MM7232	5310 to 3610	04.06.97	07.12.04
ZG768	MM7233	5304 to 3623	23.04.97	07.12.04

Italy was the only other user of the Tornado F.3, taking some twenty-four aircraft under lease as a stop-gap between the end of the F-104S-ASA Starfighter and the arrival of the Eurofighter EF.2000. 36 Stormo was the first to equip with the type in 1995 and six of their aircraft are seen here at RAF Waddington during Exercise JOTAM 2000 in the October of that year.

Not sporting overly attractive markings, MM7232, the former ZG735, is seen in employ of 53 Stormo in June 1997.

In a basic RAF colour scheme MM55060/3630, one of four twin-stickers taken on loan, is seen landing at RAF Waddington during Exercise JOTAM 2000. The jet was the former ZE208 and had originally been assigned to 53 Stormo but was transferred to the Gioia-based 36 Stormo upon unit deactivation. At the end of the lease period it returned to the UK to be withdrawn and utilised for spares reclamation.

CHAPTER 21

AIRCRAFT SERVICE DETAILS

Sporting a mixture of markings, codes and styles, this nine-ship formation led by No. 111 Squadron on 13 June 2008 was for HM the Queen's Birthday Flypast.

Tornado ADV Prototypes

ZA254 AA001	Rolled out 09.08.79. First flight 27.10.79 with Eagles and Kenward. BAe trials aircraft until retired and then to RAF Coningsby where it was used for ground training as 9253M.
ZA267 AB001	First flight 18.07.80 ('twin-stick' variant) with Millett and Kenward; BAe/A&AEE trials aircraft. Retired by January 1998 and placed into store at Boscombe Down. Delivered to RAF Marham for ground training as 9284M and still current (as of 08.10).
ZA283 AC001	First flight 18.11.80 with Gordon-Johnson and Hurst. BAe development aircraft and later becoming the Typhoon chase aircraft for ZH590 which first flew on 14.03.97. Retired in 2000 and flown to St Athan on 18.01.00 for storage. Fuselage noted Pickerston dump in 11.90 and finally scrapped in 01.01. Fin had been removed and fitted to ZD940.

Tornado F.2

ZD899 AT00I	First flew 12.04.84 with Eric Bucklow and Les Hurst. BAe trials aircraft until delivered to Boscombe Down for storage on 30.06.04.
ZD900 AT002	First flew 05.03.84. BAe/A&AEE trials aircraft as part of the DTEO/FJTS. Flown back to Warton in 02.96 to donate its centre fuselage section to replace that on ZE343. Returned to St Athan by 03.97 where the sectioned airframe was noted. Rear was scrapped in 01.01 and the forward section sent to RAF Lossiemouth for armament training. Original centre fuselage from ZE343 sent to Conifer Metals on 12.12.02 for disposal.
ZD901 ATO03	First flew 14.06.84. Delivered to Coningsby (first Tornado ADV for the RAF) 05.11.84 as 'AA'/229 OCU. Recoded as 'AB'/229 OCU during 07.87. Flown to St Athan for storage19.10.87. Gave up centre fuselage to replace that on ZE154 in 10.94. Sectioned fuselage noted at St Athan between 05.98 and 10.00 but centre and rear scrapped in 01.01. Forward fuselage to RAF Brize Norton on 13.08.01 for C-17 load trials, returning to St Athan in 09.01 and dumped by 04.02. Disposed of for scrapping on 07.08.02 and remains noted at Conifer Metals, Clay Cross in 11.02.
ZD902 AT004	First flew 04.09.84. Delivered to Coningsby 10.05.85. To 'AC'/229 OCU that month. To RAE Farnborough 24.04.88, and was operational with the RAE's Experimental Flying Squadron by mid-'91 as the 'Tornado Integrated Avionics Research Aircraft' (TIARA).

The first production Tornado F.2 ZD899 undertook a considerable amount of early development work on behalf of both BAE Systems and MBDA in missile development and integration. This company head-on shot with flaps and slats down profiles the aircraft's cross-section and it can be seen armed with four Skyflash and two AIM-9 sidewinder missiles.

ZD903 AT005	First flew 21.09.84. Delivered to Coningsby 05.11.84 as 'AB'/229 OCU. To St Athan for storage 16.11.87. Taken to Warton in 02.96 where it donated its centre fuselage to ZE728 with sectioned airframe returned to St Athan for further storage. Rear scrapped in 01.01 and forward fuselage used for armament training but dumped by 08.02 and disposed of to Conifer Metals, Clay Cross, in 12.12.02.
ZD904 AT006	First flew 30.01.85. Delivered to Coningsby 24.05.85 and became 'AE' with 229 OCU that month. To St Athan for storage by 01.88. Centre fuselage given up to ZE759 and remains dumped in 03.00 and finally scrapped in 01.01.
ZD905 AS001	First flew 11.01.85. Delivered to Boscombe Down 19.02.85. With A&AEE 'A' Sqn during 04.85. Flown to Coningsby 21.10.85 and became 'AV'/229 OCU by 11.85; to St Athan store mid-'87 (no fin by 09.93). Delivered to Warton in 02.96 and centre fuselage donated to ZE258. Sectioned fuselage back at St Athan by 08.97 and rear scrapped in 01.01. Forward fuselage used for BDRT in 01.02 but dumped by 08.02 and disposed of to Conifer Metals, Clay Cross, on 12.12.02.
ZD906 AS002	First flew 05.02.85. Delivered to Coningsby 10.05.85, becoming 'AN'/229 OCU that month. Flown to St Athan for storage 03.86. Gave up centre fuselage to ZE294 and sectioned fuselage noted dumped at St Athan on 17.01.00, although forward section later delivered to RAF Leuchars for BDRT.
ZD932 AS003	First flew 22.03.85. Delivered to Coningsby 29.04.85, taking up the code 'AM' with 229 OCU by 06.85. To St Athan for storage 11.03.87. Donated centre fuselage to ZE255 and sectioned remains used in BDRT until at least 06.02.
ZD933 AS004	First flew 16.04.85. Delivered to St Athan 10.01.86 for engineering familiarisation, being placed in storage there on 13.03.86 (fin removed by 11.93). Donated centre fuselage to ZE729 with section fuselage returning to St Athan for further storage by 05.98 until passing into hands of NDT School until at least 06.02. Disposed of as scrap on 27.02.03.
ZD934 AT007	First flew 17.04.85. Delivered to Coningsby 20.05.85, becoming 'AD'/229 OCU that month. Flown to St Athan for storage 25.09.86, remaining as such until 11.99. Donated centre fuselage to ZE786 and remains dumped on 12.10.00. Centre and rear sections scrapped in 01.01 and forward fuselage to RAF Leeming for armament training.
ZD935 AT008	First flew 16.05.85. Delivered to Coningsby 21.06.85, becoming 'AF' with 229 OCU by 08.85. To Empire Test Pilots School, Boscombe Down early 1988. Noted at Coningsby 03.92, reportedly in use as a weapons load trainer until 1996. Returned to Warton in 02.96 and donated centre fuselage to ZE793 with remains returning to St Athan by 04.98. Rear section dumped 01.00, whilst forward fuselage and ZE786 centre section, with rear from ZE210, sent to Shawbury on 22.03.00. Original rear scrapped 01.01 and fuselage to Conifer Metals, Clay Cross, 23.04.02.
ZD936 AS005	First flew 14.06.85. Delivered to Coningsby 26.07.85 and used as a 'spares-ship' until 02.86 when noted operational as 'AP'/229 OCU. To St Athan for storage 04.03.87 (fin removed by 09.93). Donated centre fuselage to ZE251. Rear section scrapped in 01.01 and forward fuselage to DERA Bedford.

The Tornado F.2 version saw very little service with the RAF, with the average operational life being a mere fifteen months. Dramatic cutbacks in defence spending saw the envisaged upgrade to F.2A standard abandoned, although they in turn contributed to a huge defence saving when they donated their centre fuselage sections to the damaged F.3s. ZD933/AO of No.229 OCU was delivered to RAF Coningsby by Eric Bucklow in May 1985 but had been retired at St Athan only ten months later.

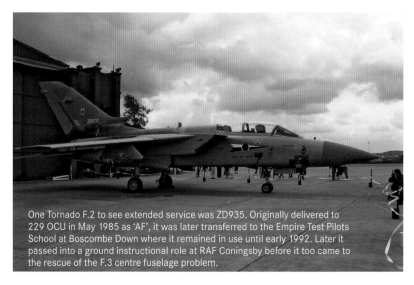

One Tornado F.2 to see extended service was ZD935. Originally delivered to 229 OCU in May 1985 as 'AF', it was later transferred to the Empire Test Pilots School at Boscombe Down where it remained in use until early 1992. Later it passed into a ground instructional role at RAF Coningsby before it too came to the rescue of the F.3 centre fuselage problem.

ZD937 AS006	First flew 28.06.85. Delivered to Coningsby 14.08.85 becoming 'AQ' with 229 OCU that same month. To St Athan for storage 08.12.86, and was in use with the BDR school during 09.93. Donated centre fuselage to ZE736 and rear section used for BDRT at St Athan. Dumped 11.00 and scrapped 01.01.
ZD938 AS007	First flew 02.08.85. Delivered to Coningsby 02.09.85 and noted as 'AR' with 229 OCU soon after. Flown to St Athan for storage 24.04.87 (fin removed by 09.93). Centre fuselage donated to ZE295 and forward and rear sections to Shawbury for storage 01.03.00 until at least 07.04.

ZD939 AS008	First flew 08.08.85. Delivered to Coningsby 18.09.85 and had become 'AS' with 229 OCU by the end of the month; placed in store at St Athan by 02.87. To Saudi Support Unit, Warton by 03.92. Donated centre fuselage to ZE292 and sectioned airframe returned to St Athan. Forward fuselage to RAF Cosford 18.02.02 and rear used for ground training at St Athan.
ZD940 AS009	First flew 19.08.85. Delivered to Coningsby 02.10.85 and took up the code 'AT' with 229 OCU that month. Flown to St Athan for storage 09.01.87 (tail removed by 09.93). Donated centre fuselage to ZE288 and sectioned fuselage return to St Athan by 05.98 until dumped 04.02 with tail fin from ZA283 attached. Disposed of to Conifer Metals, Clay Cross, 09.09.02.
ZD941 AS010	First flew 02.09.85. Delivered to Coningsby 09.10.85 (final F.2 variant) and became 'AU'/229 OCU that same month. Arrived at St Athan for storage 09.01.87. Centre fuselage donated to ZE254 and sectioned remains noted at St Athan 04.98 but dumped by 03.00 and scrapped 01.01.

Tornado F.3

ZE154 AT009	First flew 20.11.85. To A&AEE 'A' Sqn for evaluation 24.12.85. Displayed at the Coningsby 'Open Day' on 14.06.86 (public debut of the F.3). Back to BAe Warton during late 1986 before delivery to Coningsby ASF 16.07.87. First noted as 'AK'/229 OCU 09.87 (No.65 Sqn marks). To St Athan by 31.08.88. Arrived Leeming 14.09.89. Noted flying unmarked with both 23 and 25 Sqn during 10.89. By 11.89 transferred to 229 OCU (still unmarked). Noted as 'AD'/229 OCU 02.90. Placed in store at St Athan following centre fuselage damage. Roaded to Warton where it received the centre fuselage from ZD901 and returned to service in 07.95 and assigned to No.43 Sqn as 'GI'. To No.56 Sqn 12.12.96 and allocated code 'AN' before loan to 111 Sqn where it operated devoid of markings. Returned to 56 Sqn as 'AN' before recoding to 'LT' in 12.01. Reassigned to 25 Sqn 06.02 but used by other Leeming squadrons. Returned to 56 Sqn by 03.04 and wfu 12.05. Dispatched to Leeming for RTP 06.01.06.
ZE155 AS011	First flew 16.10.86. BAe JTIDS trials aircraft (deployed to MCAS Yuma, Arizona, USA 09.87). Returned to Warton from Yuma via Goose Bay on 27.09.87, becoming the first British fighter to carry out an unrefuelled transatlantic crossing (flying time 4 hours 45 minutes). Noted with A&AEE 'A' Sqn during 06.90 but retained as part of BAE Systems test fleet until dispatched to Leeming on 25.05.06 for spares recovery.
ZE156 AS012	First flew 06.02.87. Delivered to 229 OCU at Coningsby 03.03.87. Noted as 'AM'/229 OCU 03.87. Became 'AV' with the unit by 11.87. To St Athan by 01.89. Noted unmarked with 23 Sqn during late 10.89. To 'FJ'/25 Sqn by 01.90. To BAe Warton during late 1990/early 1991. Noted uncoded with 43 Sqn 09.92, still wearing 25 Sqn marks. Transferred to 111 Sqn by 05.93, becoming 'HE' by the following month. Recoded 'E' with revised toned-down unit insignia until transfer to 56 Sqn as 'UX' by 04.02. To 'GA'/43 Sqn 08.04 but back with 56 Sqn by 03.05 and assigned 'WA'. Received 2005 Tornado F.3 display markings in 05.05 which it retained until being placed in store at Leeming on 26.01.07 prior to spares reclamation.
ZE157 AT010	First flew 14.01.86. To A&AEE 'A' Sqn 25.04.86. Returned to BAe Warton. Delivered to Coningsby 25.09.86, becoming 'AH' with 229 OCU 10.86. To St Athan 07.88, being re-delivered to Coningsby 18.07.89. To 'BF'/29 Sqn during 08.89. To 'CM'/5 Sqn during 02.91. To 'AB'/229 OCU early 03.91. Noted with 43 Sqn as 'AB'/no marks during 06.91. Recoded 'AI'/56 Sqn 01.94 before becoming 'BY'/29 Sqn. To 'GK'/43 Sqn by 10.98 but back with 56 Sqn (still in 43 marks) in 10.00 until transfer to 25 Sqn in 10.02. Recoded 'TY' 10.03 and transferred to 56 Sqn by 05.05 although loaned back to 25 Sqn 04.06. Transferred to 43 Sqn shortly afterwards, remaining on strength until transfer to Leeming for spares reclamation on 27.07.09.
ZE158 AS013	First flew 25.09.86. Delivered to 229 OCU at Coningsby 30.10.86 (unmarked). Noted as 'AK'/229 OCU 02.87, then as 'AP'/229 OCU 08.87. To St Athan 04.08.88, next noted unmarked with 25 Sqn during 03.90 (receiving code 'FK' by 09.90). Joined Leuchars wing 29.10.90. Deployed to Dhahran 18.11.90, coded 'D' with 43 [C] Sqn. Returned to the UK (Leeming) during 02.91, and was operating (still coded 'D') with 11 Sqn by 05.03.91. Noted as 'DC'/11 Sqn 04.91, although was operated for a time as such by 23 Sqn. Damaged in mid-air collision (with ZE159) 01 16.07.92. Repaired at Leeming returning to 11 Sqn strength. Transferred to 'HZ'/111 Sqn by 10.97 but recoded with toned down markings as 'Z' in 08.98 the first aircraft of the unit to be so marked. With 56 Sqn in 05.02 and 11 Sqn in 10.02. Deployed to Gulf during the second Gulf campaign, returning with 111 Sqn in 04.03. To 'FF'/25 Sqn by 01.07 returning to 111 Sqn by 03.08 and assigned code 'HG'. Placed in store at Leuchars in 11.08 still as 'FF'/25 Sqn and transferred to Leeming on 22.01.09 for RTP.
ZE159 AS014	First flew 27.06.86. Delivered to Coningsby 29.07.86, becoming 'AW/229 OCU by 08.86. Flown to St Athan 12.01.88, returning to Coningsby during 02.90. Switched to 25 Sqn as 'FC' by 07.90. Became 'DO'/11 [C] Sqn by 24.08.90 and deployed to Dhahran 22.09.90. Noted as 'O'/43 [C] Sqn by early 1991. Returned to the UK (Leeming) 12.02.91 and joined 11 Sqn (still as 'O') by 19.02.91. Became 'EC'/23 Sqn 05.91. Damaged in mid-air collision (with ZE158) 16.07.92. Repaired and took up the code 'EG' with 23 Sqn by 09.92. Deployed to Malaysia for IADS '92' 09.92. Deployed to Gioia del Colle 19.04.93 under Operation Grapple (returned to Leeming during 05.93). Reassigned as 'DA'/11 Sqn then 'DE' until transfer to 111 Sqn by 04.97 where it was allocated the code 'HR'. Became 'Q'/111 Sqn in 11.98. Recoded 'R' and then 'ZW' (applied in error) before becoming 'UV' in 10.01. Received 111 Sqn special markings with black tail in 09.02. To 56 Sqn 03.03, still in special marks, although had returned to 111 Squadron by the September. Airframe later stored at St Athan in 01.07 until disposed of to Prestons at Potto, Northumberland, in 10.07.

ZE160 AT011	First flew 02.07.86. Delivered to Coningsby 08.08.86, becoming 'AG'/229 OCU later that month. To St Athan 08.04.88, and flew from there to Leeming on 09.08.90 to become 'EH'/23 Sqn by 12.08.90. Transferred to Leuchars and became 'HA'/111 Sqn 09.90 to take part in the 'Battle of Britain 50th Anniversary Flypast' on 15.09.90 (none of the unit's original aircraft were available due to Operation Granby). Noted unmarked 10.01.91 at Leeming, becoming 'DZ'/11 Sqn by 16.01.91. Arrived at Coningsby 13.03.91 (still coded 'Z') as part of 29 Sqn's return from the Gulf (it is thought that the aircraft had only come from at Decimomannu and did not deploy to Dhahran). Became 'BY'/29 Sqn during 04.91. To Leuchars (still as 'BY') 05.92, operating with 111 Sqn. To 23 Sqn as 'EX' by the end of 03.93. Took part in the static line-up for the Royal Review at Marham 01.04.93. To 'DV'/11 Sqn 04.94 and first aircraft to receive revised unit markings in 07.99 with nose-bars relocated to fin and double eagle reduced in size but superimposed on a yellow disc. Recoded 'TX' 05.01 to 25 Sqn by 08.01 and 56 Sqn 10.02. With 111 Sqn so marked in 08.05.
ZE161 AS015	First flew 07.07.86. Delivered to Coningsby 01.08.86. To 'AX'/229 CU by late 08.86. To 'DX'/11 Sqn 05.88 (maintenance trainer at Leeming prior to the squadron's re-formation). To St Athan. Next noted unmarked in the Leuchars ASF 05.90. To 'GI'/43 Sqn by 07.90. Transferred to Leeming 22.08.90, becoming 'DN'/11[C] Sqn by 05.09.90. Delivered to Leuchars on 24.09.90 still coded as 'DN', and was soon operating with 43 Sqn (uncoded by early 11.90). Deployed to Dhahran (unmarked) 11.01.91, becoming 'R'/43 [C] Sqn in theatre. Returned to Leeming during 02.91. Noted as 'R' 04.91, operating with 25 Sqn. Became 'FG'/25 Sqn 06.91. Noted flying unmarked with 25 Sqn during 03.93, before switching to Coningsby during 05.93. To 'HD'/111 Sqn then 'DQ'/11 Sqn in 10.97. Loaned to AWC and then 43 Sqn in 06.98. With 5 Sqn 11.98 but back with 11 Sqn as 'DQ' before transfer to 'UU'/43 Sqn 02.02. Deployed to Dhahran during the second Gulf campaign and named 'Lacey' with 28 alongside artwork which depicted four Ace playing cards on the starboard side of the nose wheel door. Nose art on the port side comprised of the 'Foghorn Leghorn' cartoon character with Union Jack tail feathers and holding a sword through a caricature of Saddam's head with the inscription 'Operation Telic 43'. On return to 43 Sqn took up code 'GB' remaining with unit but noted unmarked in 03.04, but fully coded in 01.05 until placed into store in 12.08. Dispatched to Leeming 16.01.09 for spares reclamation.
ZE162 AS016	First flew 16.07.86. Delivered to Coningsby 13.08.86. To 'AY'/229 OCU 09.86. To St Athan 20.11.87. Flown to Coningsby and became 'AW'/229 OCU during 03.90. To Leeming 19.08.90, becoming 'DM'/11 [C] Sqn by 06.09.90. Deployed to Dhahran 16.09.90. Returned to the UK (Leeming) 12.01.91, becoming 'M'/11 Sqn by 16.1.91. To 'FK'/25 Sqn 05.91. Loaned to 29 Sqn 10.92. Noted flying unmarked in 05.96. Recoded 'UR' in 05.02 with 5 Sqn. Deployed to Dhahran for the second Gulf campaign where it received the name 'Proctor' and 54 alongside artwork depicting four Ace playing cards on starboard side of nosewheel door. Returned to Leuchars with 111 Sqn and assigned the code 'HM'. Placed in store at Leuchars 12.08 and flown to Leeming on 20.02.09 for spares reclamation.

ZE163 AT012	First flew 06.07.87. Delivered to Coningsby 11.09.87. To 'AL'/29 OCU by 10.87. To St Athan by 07.88, returned to Coningsby by 12.88 when seen operating unmarked with 29 Sqn. To 'CF'/5 Sqn by 06.90. Deployed to Dhahran 11.08.90, returning to the UK during 09.90. Noted with 111 Sqn 01.91 still as 'CF' to 'A2'/229 OCU by 07.91. Became 'AA'/229 OCU 03.92 (no marks). Noted at St Athan during 05.93 following 'CAT 3' damage. Reported that it would receive rear fuselage from ZG753, which itself had been returned to St Athan with damage in 05.97, but not known whether this actually occurred. Noted on air test 07.01 and assigned to 111 Sqn as 'TW'. With 43 Sqn in 10.02 and loaned to FJTS at Boscombe Down then 56 Sqn. Back with 43 Sqn by 03.09 but transferred to 111 Sqn at disbandment. Assigned code 'HY' in 07.09 and fully painted by end of year.
ZE164 AS017	First flew 22.07.86. Delivered to Coningsby 18.09.86 and became 'AN'/229 OCU by 10.86. To 'AU'/229 OCU 01.88. Flown to St Athan by 01.89. To Leeming, and became 'EH'/23 Sqn by 12.89. To St Athan once again during 03.90. Flown to Leuchars during 05.90 and to 'HH'/111 Sqn 08.90. Transferred to Leeming 03.08.90, becoming 'DQ'/11[C] Sqn by 06.09.90. Noted at Leuchars late 09.90. Deployed to Dhahran 18.11.90 (unmarked). Noted in theatre as 'G'/43[C] Sqn during '90. Returned to UK mid-03.91 and noted as 'G'/11 Sqn 04.91. Became 'DA'/11 Sqn 05.91. Deployed to Gioia del Colle 19.04.93 as part of Operation Grapple (retuned to Leeming during 05.93). Transferred to 'HQ'/111 Sqn by 10.97 but back with 11 Sqn unmarked by 01.99. Allocated code 'DA' but doubtful ever carried. Became 'UQ'/5 Sqn 07.02 before transfer to 43 Sqn in 05.03. Coded 'GD' by 11.04 until placed in storage at Leuchars in 11.05. Re-allocated to 111 Sqn in 03.07 eventually taking up the code 'HO'.
ZE165 AS018	First flew 11.08.86. Delivered to Coningsby 08.09.86 and noted as 'AZ'/229 OCU 02.87. Flown to St Athan early 04.88. Flown to Leuchars and noted with 111 Sqn (still as 'AZ') during 05.90. Became 'HL'/111 Sqn 08.90. Transferred to Leeming by 10.09.90 as 'DU'/11 [C] Sqn. Acted as a Granby deployment airspare 16.09.90, actually deploying to Dhahran 22.09.90. Noted in theatre as 'U'/43[C] Sqn 01.91. Returned to the UK (Leeming) 12.02.91 and was operating with 11 Sqn the next day (still coded 'U'). Transferred to Coningsby by late 02.91 and noted operating with 5 Sqn (again, still carrying the 'U' code). Became 'A' by 04.91, operating with 29 Sqn, although the aircraft was loaned to 11 Sqn at Leeming during the month. Became 'BJ'/29 Sqn 05.91. Noted flying with 25 Sqn during 04.93, becoming 'FO' by 06.93. Recoded 'ZK' during 1997 with whom it received modified unit marks with the silver nose and tail bars outlined in a thicker black band with the code presented in black until transfer to Leuchars as 'Q'/111 Sqn in 12.98. Loaned to F3OEU in 05.99 until 07.99. Transferred as 'UP'/43 Sqn by 05.02 until recoded 'GE'. Again loaned to FJWOEU in 04.04 and 11 Sqn in 08.04, still marked as 'GE'. Transferred to 111 Sqn before being flown to RAF Shawbury for storage on 25.04.08 and still current 10.10.
ZE166 AT013	First flew 27.10.86. Delivered to Coningsby 12.11.86, becoming 'AI' with 229 OCU that month. To St Athan for attention 28.03.88. Flown to Coningsby, becoming 'CT'/5 Sqn by 08.89. To 'AF'/229 OCU 01.90. Involved in a mid-air collision with ZE862 on 10.01.96, both aircraft crashing in vicinity of Sleaford.

ZE167 AS019	First flew 02.10.86. Delivered to Coningsby 23.10.86, taking up the code 'AL' with 229 OCU during 11.86. To 'AR'/229 OCU 09.87. To St Athan for attention during 04.88, returning to Coningsby by 02.91. Noted in 25 Sqn/special marks during 04.91 for the 1991 air display season (consisting of black and silver fin, with a silver cheat-line edged in black applied to each side of the lower fuselage). Transferred to 111 Sqn (still in 25 Sqn special marks) during 11.91. Became 'HM'/111 Sqn 01.92. To BAe/A&AEE by 05.93 for unspecified trials. Returned to Leuchars and recoded 'HX' at some point. Transferred to AMI in 03.97 as MM7234/5314 with whom it received special Tiger Squadron markings which were retained after transfer to 36 Stormo as 3624. Returned to St Athan 31.03.04 at end of lease period for spares recovery and disposed of for scrapping on 03.11.04.
ZE168 AS020	First flew 31.10.86. Delivered to Coningsby 18.11.86, becoming 'AO'/229 OCU by 02.87. To St Athan 28.03.88. Noted unmarked at Leeming during 09.90. Transferred to 111 Sqn (still unmarked) 01.91. Noted as 'N'/no marks with 11 Sqn 03.91, transferring to 23 Sqn as such by the following month. Became 'EB'/23 Sqn by 05.91. Took part in IADS '92 during 09.92. Loaned to 5 Sqn 07.09.93–11.93. With F3OEU 10.01 where it undertook ASRAAM firing trials at Eglin AFB in 04.02 becoming the only known Tornado F.3 to have achieved air-to-air kills, bringing down two QF4Es. Recoded 'UN' in 02.02. To 11 Sqn 06.03 and received code 'DN' by 09.04. With 25 Sqn in 06.05 and 43 Sqn in 04.06 but back with 25 Sqn as 'FA' in 10.06. Transferred to 'HH'/111 Sqn 07.09.
ZE199 ATO14	First flew 19.11.86. Delivered to Coningsby 22.12.86. Noted as 'AJ'/229 OCU 02.87. Became the first Tornado F.3 to land at Leeming following the station's re-opening on 11.01.88. To St Athan 03.03.88, flown to Leeming 10.05.90. To 'DQ'/11 Sqn by 07.90. Loaned to 111 Sqn 30.08.90. Noted unmarked at Leeming 18.01.91, although the code 'W' was applied one week later when the aircraft was noted operating unmarked with 11 Sqn. Noted as 'W' with 43 [C] Sqn when that unit returned to the UK (Leuchars) from the Gulf via Decimomannu on 13.03.91 (believed to have deployed to the theatre during 02.91). Transferred to 25 Sqn (still as 'W') during 04.91, becoming 'FL' during the following month. To 'AI'/56 Sqn by 06.99 (still marked as 'FL') on loan to 43 Sqn similarly marked before permanent transfer as 'L'/111 Sqn in 05.01. Back with 56 [R] Sqn 10.01 and coded 'TV' by 01.02. Flown to Leeming in 2005 for storage and eventual spares reclamation.
ZE200 AS021	First flew 24.02.87. Delivered to Coningsby 06.03.87. To A&AEE for trials 05.87. Noted as 'AS'/229 OCU 09.87. Transferred to 5 Sqn as 'CI' by 10.88. By 06.90 operating unmarked with 229 OCU, and became 'AV' 07.90. To Leeming 03.09.90, becoming 'DZ'/11 [C] Sqn by 12.09.90. Noted at Leuchars 26.09.90, and operating uncoded with 43 Sqn by end of 10.90. Deployed to Dhahran 18.11.90. Noted as 'L' with 43 [C] Sqn 01.91. Operating with 11 Sqn (still as 'L'/no marks) during 04.91. To 'DB'/11 Sqn 05.91. Damaged and sent to St Athan for repairs and next noted with 25 Sqn in 11.98 still marked as 'DB'/11 Sqn although with squadron insignia. Recoded 'UM' and fully marked as 5 Sqn by 07.01. To 111 Sqn by 02.02, although loaned to 25 Sqn in 06.02. Uncoded with 111 Sqn in 10.05 but allocated code 'HN'. Fully marked by 01.10.
ZE201 AS022	First flew 04.12.86. Delivered to Coningsby 17.12.86. To 'AO'/229 OCU by 02.87. To St Athan for attention (noted there 06.89). Flown to Leeming 10.01.91 following attention at Warton. Flying as 'E' with 11 Sqn by 22.01.91. Noted operating with 43 [C] Sqn (still as 'E') when the unit returned to the UK (Leuchars) from Dhahran on 13.03.91 (the aircraft had deployed to Dhahran during 02.91). Noted flying with 23 Sqn as 'E' during 04.91, becoming 'ED' with that unit during 05.91. Deployed to Gioia del Colle under Operation Grapple 19.04.93. 'GA'/43 Sqn in 01.99 but recoded 'UL' in 05.02 on transfer to 56 [R] Sqn. To 25 Sqn 06.03, becoming 'FB' sometime later, so noted in 07.06. Transferred to 'HU'/111 Sqn 02.08 and current.
ZE202 AT015	First flew 26.08.86. Delivered to Coningsby 12.09.86 (unmarked). Noted with A&AEE/BAe 06.88. To 229 OCU as 'AH' 07.88. To St Athan 21.02.90, although it had returned to Coningsby by the end of 03.90. To 'AG'/56 [R] Sqn (229 OCU marks) 02.93. Leased to AMI 08.95 as MM55056/3601 before recoding to 3620. Returned to St Athan at end of lease period for spares recovery. Eventually disposed of to M. Williams & Son, Hitchin for scrap on 22.09.07.
ZE203 AS023	First flew 29.08.86. Delivered to Coningsby 01.10.86. To 'AO'/229 OCU by 10.86. To 29 Sqn as 'BA' 04.87; reverted to 'AO'/229 OCU by early 08.88, flown to St Athan by 01.89. Next noted with 25 Sqn as 'FI' 10.89. To St Athan once again on 08.01.90. To 43 Sqn as 'GD' during early 08.90. To Leeming 14.08.90, becoming 'DA' with 11 [C] Sqn by 26.08.90 (acted as airspare for the Granby deployment on 29.08.90). Deployed to Dhahran 23.09.90. Recoded as 'A' in theatre by 43 [C] Sqn; returned to the UK (Coningsby) 14.03.91. Noted flying with 11 Sqn (still as 'A') during late 03.91, passing to 25 Sqn as such by the following month. To 'FI'/25 Sqn during 05.91. Loaned to 111 Sqn during 03.92. Deployed to Alaska for 'Distant Frontier 92' on 06.04.92. Returned to 25 Sqn during 05.92. Recoded 'UK' by 07.01 and noted unmarked with 5 Sqn in 05.02 and later with 11 Sqn in 10.03. Became 'DE'/11 Sqn by 05.04 and to 43 Sqn in 11.05 becoming 'GA' by 10.06. Loaned to Qinetiq 12.12.07 and current.

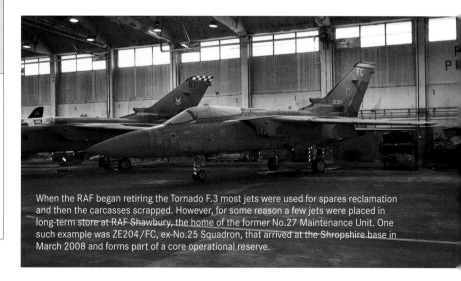

When the RAF began retiring the Tornado F.3 most jets were used for spares reclamation and then the carcasses scrapped. However, for some reason a few jets were placed in long-term store at RAF Shawbury, the home of the former No.27 Maintenance Unit. One such example was ZE204/FC, ex-No.25 Squadron, that arrived at the Shropshire base in March 2008 and forms part of a core operational reserve.

ZE204 AS024	First flew 10.09.86. Delivered to Coningsby 14.10.86. Operating unmarked with 229 OCU during 10.86. To 'BB'/29 Sqn by 05.87. Reportedly to 'AT'/229 OCU during 08.88, although had reverted to 'BB'/29 Sqn prior to dispatch to St Athan during 11.88. Noted back with 229 OCU, as 'AV', by 10.89. To 43 Sqn as 'GJ' 07.90. To Leeming on 23.08.90, joining 11 [C] Sqn as 'DB' 26.08.90. Deployed to Dhahran 16.09.90. Recoded as 'B' by 43 [C] Sqn in theatre, and possibly returned to the UK (Coningsby) on 13.03.91. Noted at Leeming during 04.91 (still as 'B'/no marks). To 'DD'/11 Sqn during 05.91. With 5 Sqn 11.98 and 43 Sqn 05.01. Recoded 'UJ' in 08.01 but still with 11 Sqn marks. With 25 Sqn 06.02 and after a period of serving as the Leeming WLT aircraft became 'FC'/25 Sqn in 11.06. Wfu at Leeming in 12.07 and flown to RAF Shawbury for storage 17.03.08, and still current 10.10
ZE205 AT016	First flew 18.09.86. Delivered to Coningsby 16.10.86. To 'AJ'/229 OCU 11.86. To 'AA'/229 OCU 06.87. To 'BS'/29 Sqn by 03.90 (still wore 229 OCU marks with the 'BS' code for a short while). Deployed to Dhahran 11.08.90 as part of 5 [C] Sqn. Returned to Coningsby 09.90, and was noted in special 29 Sqn 75th anniversary marks during 11.90 (consisting of a black spine/fin leading edge, with three red 'X's superimposed atop the fin. Next was a yellow band following the fin top and forward contours with a red '75' inscription, and finally a smaller red band also following the same contour. Nose-bars, also of three 'X's, were applied either side of the roundel). To 'AA'/229 OCU 02.91. Noted unmarked with 56 [R] Sqn 08.92, becoming 'AM' with that unit by 10.92. Leased to AMI as MM55061/5312 before transfer to 36 Stormo as 3620. Returned to St Athan at end of lease period on 28.07.04 for spares recovery and eventually scrapped in 01.05.
ZE206 AS025	First flew 05.11.86. Delivered to Coningsby 28.04.87. To 'BF'/29 Sqn 05.87. Loaned to 229 OCU during 09.88. To St Athan by 01.89, then to 'GG'/43 Sqn by 01.90. Flown back to St Athan 23.03.90. Arrived at Leeming 15.08.90, becoming 'DC' with 11 [C] Sqn 26.08.90. Deployed to Dhahran 29.08.90. Became 'C' with 43 [C] Sqn whilst in theatre. Returned to the UK mid-03.91. Noted as 'B' with 23 Sqn during late 03.91, taking up the 'EW' code with the unit during 04.91. Loaned to 111 Sqn during 03.92. Deployed to Eielson AFB, Alaska 06.04.92 as part of Exercise Distant Frontier 92. Returned to 23 Sqn 05.92. Deployed to Malaysia as part of 'IADS 92' during 09.92. To 'FH'/25 Sqn (but never carried the code) before re-locating to 43 Sqn as 'GL'. Returned to 25 Sqn 02.99 still as 'FH' although code smaller in black and re-positioned to nearer leading edge of fin, until recoded 'UI' in 10.01. To 111 Sqn and deployed to Dhahran for the second Gulf campaign, returning in 04.03 to 43 Sqn. Loaned to BAE Systems as part of test fleet 11.04 but returned to 43 Sqn on 17.04.08. Placed in store at Leuchars 05.09 until flown to Leeming 18.06.09 for spares reclamation.
ZE207 AS026	First flew 07.09.87. Delivered to Coningsby 23.10.87. To 'AK'/229 OCU by 12.87. To 'BL'/29 Sqn by 01.88, becoming 'BJ' by 11.88. To St Athan by 01.90. Operated with 229 OCU (still as 'BJ'/29 Sqn marks) during 07.90. To 'CK'/5 Sqn by late 02.91, transferring to 11 Sqn during 03.91 (still as 'CK'). To 43 Sqn as 'GC' during 06.91. Incurred a bird strike and noted with TASF in 10.02. Reassigned to 56 [R] Sqn 02.03 as 'UH'. Received the 'Firebirds 2003' fin tip marks in 05.03. Transferred back to 43 Sqn and recoded 'GC' in 06.04. To Leeming in 2005 for RTP.

ZE208 AT017	First flew 27.11.86. Delivered to Coningsby 16.12.86. To 'BT'/29 Sqn by 30.03.87. Operating with 229 OCU during 06.88. To 'BR'/29 Sqn by mid-08.88, although reverted once again to 229 OCU charge by 11.88, taking up the code 'AK' during 12.88. Noted unmarked at Leeming during 02.90, becoming 'DZ' with 11 Sqn 04.90. To 'BS'/29 Sqn by 08.90. Noted unmarked with 56 [R] Sqn 08.92, becoming 'AN' with the unit by 11.92. Leased to AMI and rolled out as MM55060/5301 on 14.12.96. On transfer to 36 Stormo became 3630 and returned to St Athan at end of lease period on 06.08.04 and placed in storage.
ZE209 AS027	First flew 21.01.87. Delivered to Coningsby 06.02.87. To 'BC'/29 Sqn 03.87. To 'AS'/229 OCU 07.88. Noted unmarked at Coningsby 07.92. Arrived at RAF Mount Pleasant, Falkland Islands 08.07.92 to become 'H'/1435 Flt (named 'Hope'). Returned to UK in 01.94 joining 56 [R] Sqn as 'AV' by 07.94. Returned to 1435 Flt as 'H' 21.10.95 but not clear when it returned to UK. Noted with 111 Sqn unmarked 04.96 but allocated code 'HZ'. To 56 [R] Sqn still unmarked and suffered an undercarriage failure on landing at Coningsby on 17.02.97 when operating as 'Scorcher 3'. Following repairs it had returned to service by 02.98 and with 5 Sqn in 03.99 where it was allocated the code 'CE'. To 56 [R] Sqn as 'AX' but loaned to 43 Sqn in 07.01 and then 111 Sqn in 02.02 still as 'AX'. To St Athan for spares recovery and centre fuselage utilised in mid-life fuselage upgrade programme. Forward and rear fuselage sections noted stored at St Athan in 01.05 and 08.05.
ZE210 AS028	First flew 27.01.87. Delivered to Coningsby 12.02.87. Noted flying with the F3OEU during 07.87. To 'AW'/229 OCU 02.88. To St Athan 23.11.88. Returned to Coningsby on 15.05.89, still marked as 'AW'/229 OCU. Noted in the Leuchars ASF during 09.89 as a maintenance trainer; made operational and became 'GL'/43 Sqn by 07.90. To Leeming on 14.08.90, becoming 'DD'/11 [C] Sqn soon after. Deployed to Dhahran 29.08.90. Returned to Leuchars via Nice (technical diversion) on 22.11.90. Noted in the Leuchars ASF 01.91. To Leeming by 21.01.91, coded 'G' and operating with 11 Sqn. Returned with 43 [C] Sqn to Leuchars from Dhahran on 13.03.91 (believed to have deployed to the Gulf during 02.91). To 25 Sqn (still as 'G') during 04.91, becoming 'FB' with the unit during 05.91. Loaned to 111 Sqn 03.92. and deployed to Alaska under "Distant Frontier 92" on 06.04.92; returned to 25 Sqn 05.92. To 43 Sqn by 01.95 and allocated code 'GD' but never carried. Involved in a mid-air collision with ZE733/GE on 30.10.95 and although recovered safely was declared to have suffered CAT 3/4 damage. However, by 07.96 has been re-catagorised as CAT 5 and SOC. Fuselage noted stored at St Athan 22.06.99 and dumped at the Pickerstone site on 19.01.00. It was finally scrapped 01.01.
ZE250 AT018	First flew 29.01.87. Delivered to Coningsby 24.02.87. To 'AP'/229 OCU by 07.87, although being operated by 29 Sqn (still as 'AP') during 08.87. To 'AF'/229 OCU 01.88. To St Athan for attention 06.88, being delivered to Leeming on 01.11.89. To 'EQ'/23 Sqn by 12.89. Passed to 111 Sqn 03.91 (still as 'EQ'/23 Sqn marks). Became 'HZ'/111 Sqn 08.91. Sustained CAT 4 damage by 07.92 following an engine fire (still in ASF 01.96). RTS at Coningsby via St Athan 22.09.97 and assigned to 'AM'/56 [R] Sqn. Recoded 'TR' by 09.02 and flown to RAF Shawbury for storage 17.03.08. Taken by road to Leeming 20.05.09 for spares reclamation.

ZE251 AS029	First flew 12.02.87. Delivered to Coningsby 24.02.87. Operating with F3OEU 07.87. To 'AX'/229 OCU 02.88. To 'DA'/11 Sqn by 01.90. To 111 Sqn 09.90 (still as 'DA'/11 Sqn), although became 'HB'/111 Sqn during 10.90. Noted unmarked with 11 Sqn 01.91, taking up the code 'J' by 28.01.91. To 'DE'/11 Sqn by 06.91. Stored St Athan by mid-'93 (damaged centre fuselage). Received CF from ZD936 and was returned to service with 43 Sqn as 'GA'. To 25 Sqn 11.98 and allocated 'FB' code. To 1435 Flt 25.09.99 as 'C' (Charity). Returned to UK 30.05.01 and re-assigned to 43 Sqn. Transferred to 'TP'/56 [R] Sqn 08.01 but with 11 Sqn in 10.02 and 111 Sqn in 10.02, coded 'UF' by 09.03. Stored at St Athan and broken up for spares by 03.06.
ZE252 AS030	First flew 04.03.87. Delivered to Coningsby 19.03.87. Operating with F3OEU 07.87. To 'AY'/229 OCU 03.88. To 111 Sqn (still as 'AY') 01.91, becoming 'HH' with the unit during 10.91. To 1435 Flt as 'C' (Charity) 03.04.95 returning to Coningsby 28.09.96. Allocated code 'AS' with 56 [R] Sqn but leased to AMI as MM7225/5302. Transferred to 36 Stormo and recoded 3604. Returned to St Athan following period of lease for spares recovery. Dumped by 10.94 and eventually disposed of as scrap to M. Williams & Son, Hitchin, on 16.11.04.
ZE253 AT019	First flew 09.03.87. Delivered to Coningsby 25.03.87 (joint BAe/OEU trials aircraft). To 'AB'/229 OCU 12.87. To 'AC'/56 [R] Sqn 07.92 (first aircraft to carry the unit's marks). Remained with unit until flown to St Athan for storage and eventual spares reclamation. Centre fuselage used in mid-life fuselage upgrade programme. Forward fuselage and rear section noted stored at St Athan in 01.05 and 08.05.
ZE254 AS031	First flew 12.03.87. Delivered to Coningsby 20.03.87. To 'BG'/29 Sqn 04.87. Took part in Operation Golden Eagle 21.8-25.10.88. Deployed to Dhahran 11.08.90 as part of 5 [C] Sqn. To 'CA'/5 Sqn 02.91. Loaned to 11 Sqn during 10.92. Stored St Athan, unmarked, by mid-'93 (centre fuselage damaged). Received 'new' centre fuselage donated by ZD941 and returned to service as 'GE'/43 Sqn by 01.96. To 56 [R] Sqn 10.96 becoming 'AW' by 01.98. To 'CW'/5 Sqn 04.01 and recoded 'UD'. Transferred to 25 Sqn 06.02 and allocated code 'FD' which it was noted carrying in 04.07. To 43 Sqn 09.07 and allocated code 'GM', but by 12.07 still marked as 'FD'/25 Sqn. Became 'GM'/43 Sqn by 02.08 and flown to Leeming 29.08.08 for spares reclamation.
ZE255 AS032	First flew 24.03.87. Delivered to Coningsby 02.04.87. To 'BH'/29 Sqn 04.87 (first to fly with the unit). Flown to Leuchars 22.02.90, and was operating with the base's squadrons during that month, although it had returned to 29 Sqn by 06.90, deployed to Dhahran 11.08.90 as part of 5 [C] Sqn. Transferred to 111 Sqn (still as 'BH') during 01.91. Noted operating as 'BH' with 43 Sqn during 06.91, although had reverted back to 111 Sqn as 'HI' by 10.91; Stored at St Athan 06.93 (centre fuselage damage). Gifted 'new' CF from ZD932 and re-assigned to 25 Sqn, becoming 'FR' by 05.96. To 56 Sqn 09.96 and allocated code 'AY'. Noted so marked 01.99 but with 5 Sqn in 09.00 and marked as 'CK' in 02.01. Recoded 'UC' and to 25 Sqn by 06.02 although back with 56 [R] Sqn in 06.05. Transferred to 'GC'/43 Sqn 02.06 and placed in store at Leuchars in 12.08. Flown to Leeming 19.01.09 for spares reclamation.

Seen late one evening is this fully armed example, ZE257, of No.43 Squadron. The jet is flying with a high alpha as it struggles to maintain station on the airliner that it has just intercepted. The Tornado F.3 was optimised for medium-level operations and altitudes above 23,000ft are decidedly uncomfortable.

ZE256 AT020	First flew 31.03.87. Delivered to Coningsby 08.04.87. Received trial 5 Sqn marks during 06.87, although did not officially join the unit until 26.11.87 when it took up the code 'CT'. Operating with 229 OCU by 04.88 (still as 'CT'). To 'AJ'/229 OCU 10.88. Before wearing 56 [R] Sqn marks. To 111 Sqn 05.95 and allocated code 'HY' but not believed to have been carried. With 29 Sqn 05.96 and assigned the code 'BX'. With 56 [R] Sqn 10.98, although loaned to 5 Sqn the following month. To 'AO'/56 Sqn 03.99 but recoded 'TP' in 05.02. In use as WLT at Leuchars in 09.04.
ZE257 AS033	First flew 14.04.87. Delivered to Coningsby 28.04.87. To 'BD'/29 Sqn by 05.87. To 'CB'/5 Sqn by 03.91, although had reverted to 'BD'/29 Sqn by 06.91. To 111 Sqn (unmarked) 03.93, becoming 'HN' with the unit by 06.93. To 11 Sqn 12.98 becoming 'DC'. To F3OEU as 'UB' 08.01 then to 43 Sqn in 05.04 becoming 'GI' by 05.05. Flown to Leeming 23.09.08 for spares reclamation.
ZE258 AS034	First flew 21.05.87. Delivered to Coningsby 12.06.87. To 'BE'/29 Sqn by 16.06.87. Deployed to Dhahran 11.08.90 as part of 5 [C] Sqn. To 'CJ'/5 Sqn 03.91, although transferred to 23 Sqn later the same month (still as 'CJ'). To 'EJ'/23 Sqn late 03.91, transferring to 111 Sqn (as 'EJ') 04.91. To 'GA'/43 Sqn by 05.91, taking up special marks for the unit's 75th anniversary. Stored St Athan by mid-'93 (centre fuselage damaged). Received 'new' centre section donated by ZD905 and returned to service at Coningsby 28.02.97. To 'AQ'/56 [R] Sqn before assigned at 5 Sqn in 10.01. To 1435 Flt as 'F' (Faith) by 03.04 and returned to UK as airfreight aboard a C-17 in 04.05. Fuselage placed in store at St Athan where noted in 03.06 and 01.07.
ZE287 AT021	First flew 01.05.87. Delivered to Coningsby 21.05.87. To 'AE'/229 OCU 06.87. Noted unmarked with 56 [R] Sqn 10.92. To 'AH'/56 [R] Sqn 11.92 (still in 229 OCU marks). Recoded 'AF' by 04.99 and then 'TO' in 07.02. To 11 Sqn 10.02 until at least 10.03. Became Leeming WLT aircraft before overhaul at St Athan in 04.05. Returned to 'TO'/56 [R] Sqn and then 43 Sqn until wfu at Leuchars on 08.08.08. Flown to Leeming for RTP during late 2008.

ZE288 AS035	First flew 05.06.87. Delivered to Coningsby 25.06.87. To 'BI'/29 Sqn 07.87. Took part in Operation Golden Eagle 21.8–25.10.88. To 111 Sqn/unmarked 04.91, although switched to 43 Sqn by 05.91. Became 'GG'/43 Sqn 08.91. Stored St Athan by mid-'93 (centre fuselage damaged). Gifted 'new' CF from ZD940 and returned to service as 'BH'/29 Sqn 04.96 following repair at Warton. To 'AT'/56 [R] Sqn 01.99, then 11 Sqn and 25 Sqn in 01.01 still as 'AT'. To 'HA'/111 Sqn by 05.04 until placed into store st Leuchars. Flown to Leeming for spares reclamation 05.08.09.
ZE289 AS036	First flew 12.06.87. Delivered to Coningsby 13.08.87. To 'BJ'/29 Sqn by 08.87. To 'BA'.29 Sqn 07.88. Deployed to Dhahran as part of 5 [C] Sqn 11.08.90. To 111 Sqn 01.91 (still as 'BA'). To 'HF'/111 Sqn 07.92, although the aircraft was damaged in a landing accident soon after when the nose wheel collapsed, flying again during 02.93. To 56 [R] Sqn as 'AV' then to 1435 Flt as 'C' (Charity) in 03.98 returning to the UK 02.10.99. Re-assigned to 'VX'/43 Sqn but operated unmarked in 02.02 and then to 111 Sqn until flown to Leeming 23.04.07 for spares reclamation.
ZE290 AT022	First flew 09.07.87. Delivered to Coningsby 02.10.87. To 'AD'/229 OCU 11.87. Noted operating unmarked with 25 Sqn 11.89. To 'FE'/25 Sqn 05.90. To 'AT'/229 OCU by 04.91, becoming 'AJ' with the unit by 03.92. To 'AD'/56 [R] Sqn 10.92 (no marks). To 5 Sqn by 12.97 becoming 'CJ'. Back to 'AG'/56 [R] Sqn 04.99 but flown to St Athan 11.09.01 for spares recovery and for the centre fuselage to be utilised in the mid-life fuselage upgrade programme. Forward and rear sections noted stored at St Athan 01.05 and 08.05 but eventually disposed of for scrap on 09.03.06.
ZE291 AS037	First flew 30.07.87. Delivered to Coningsby 18.09.87. To 'BK'/29 Sqn 09.87. To 'AZ'/229 OCU 04.88. Transferred to 111 Sqn ('AZ'/unmarked) 05.92. To 43 Sqn by 01.93. Stored out of use in the Leuchars ASF from mid-1993 (damage to forward fuselage). Returned to service as 'GQ'/43 Sqn by 11.97 until recoded post 12.02. To 1435 Flt by C-17 09.01.04, becoming 'D' (Desperation). Returned to UK 04.05 by same method of transport and taken by road from Brize Norton to St Athan on 26.04.05. Wfu and sold for scrap following spares reclamation. Taken to Metal & Waste Recycling during 03.06.
ZE292 AS038	First flew 06.08.87. Delivered to Coningsby 25.09.87. To 'CA'/5 Sqn by 25.11.87. Operating with 229 OCU 06.88, still as 'CA'. To 'AU'/229 OCU 09.88. Passed to 111 Sqn during 01.91 (still as 'AU'), although had returned to 229 OCU during 02.91. Transferred once again to 111 Sqn as 'AU' by 05.93, becoming 'HA' by 07.93. Stored St Athan by 09.93 (centre fuselage damaged). 'New' CF donated by ZD939 and returned to service with 56 [R] Sqn 02.12.96. Allocated code 'AZ' but not clear whether carried. Became 'AG' by 04.99 and then later recoded 'YY'. To 11 Sqn by 06.02 and 25 Sqn 05.03 where it was assigned the code 'FE' and so marked 07.07. Back with 56 [R] Sqn 01.08 and placed in store at Leuchars 05.09. Flown to Leeming for spares reclamation during 07.09.
ZE293 AT023	First flew 26.08.87. Delivered to Coningsby 09.10.87. To 'AC'/229 OCU 11.87. Transferred to 111 Sqn (still as 'AC') 08.92 (allocated the code 'HT'). Loaned to A&AEE 10.97 and alternated between Coningsby and Boscombe Down on several occasions up until 07.99. Placed on strength of F3OEU by 09.99, it was later transferred to 'TL'/56 [R] Sqn. To 'GZ'/43 Sqn by 06.04 it was wfu at Leeming in 10.05 for spares reclamation.

ZE294 AS039	First flew 18.09.87. Delivered to Coningsby 19.10.87. To 'CB'/5 Sqn 01.88, although operating unmarked with 229 OCU by 04.88. To 'AQ'/229 OCU 06.88. To 'AQ'/56 [R] Sqn 07.92; stored St Athan from mid-'93 (centre fuselage damaged). Gifted 'new' CF by ZD906 and returned to service as 'AS'/56 [R] Sqn 09.10.98. Recoded 'YK' with 25 Sqn in 06.02 before transfer as 'DD'/11 Sqn by 01.04. Wfu at Leeming during 11.05 and taken to St Athan by 01.07.
ZE295 AS040	First flew 01.10.87. Delivered to Coningsby 19.10.87. To 'CC'/5 Sqn 10.87. To 'AR'/229 OCU 7.88. To 'AW'/56[R] Sqn 04.93; withdrawn from use in 06.93 (centre fuselage damaged), being utilised as a ground trainer at Coningsby during 11.93. Gifted a 'new' CF by ZD938 and repaired at Warton in 04.96. Assigned as 'CF'/5 Sqn in 05.96 but to 'AV'/56 [R] Sqn in 08.96. To 'CA'/5 Sqn 06.00 although returned to 56 [R] Sqn as 'AY' in 02.01. With 25 Sqn during 06.02 and 11 Sqn in 10.03. Became 'DC' with latter by 01.04 although back with 25 Sqn in 10.05. Loaned to FJWOEU in 11.05 and used at WLT trainer at Leeming before being wfu in 09.07 for spares reclamation.
ZE296 AT024	First flew 27.09.87. Delivered to Coningsby 19.10.87. To 'AM'/229 OCU 11.87. To St Athan 08.02.90, returning to Coningsby (as 'AM'/229 OCU) during 05.90. Became 'GR'/43 Sqn during 10.93. To 'AD'/56 [R] Sqn by 09.98 but stored at St Athan on 11.09.01 for centre fuselage to be used in mid-life fuselage upgrade. Forward and rear sections noted stored in 01.05 and 08.05 before finally being dispatched for scrap on 14.03.06.
ZE338 AS041	First flew 09.10.87. Delivered to Coningsby 26.10.87. To 'CD'/5 Sqn 01.88, although unmarked with the unit by 04.88. To 'BB'/29 Sqn by 06.88. Deployed to Dhahran as part of 5 [C] Sqn on 11.08.90. Noted with 111 Sqn 01.91 (still as 'BB'). To 'HG'/111 Sqn by 12.91. Loaned to 25 Sqn during 05.92 but returned to 111 Sqn and reported as recoded 'G' by 01.95 but as 'HG' again in 01.98. Noted flying unmarked in 09.00 with Leuchars wing. Recoded again in 09.02 as 'YV' and to 43 Sqn in 10.03. Coded 'GJ' by 04.05 and remained with Sqn until placed into store at Leuchars in 7.09. Flown to Leeming for RTP 03.09.09.
ZE339 AS042	First flew 08.10.87. Delivered to Coningsby 26.10.87. To 'CE'/5 Sqn 12.87. To 'AN'/2290CU5.88. To 'AO'/2290CU 11.88. To 'AX'/229 OCU 04.90. To 25 Sqn/special marks 06.92 for 1992 display season. To 'FO'/25 Sqn 03.93. Took part in the Royal Review static display at Marham on 01.04.93. Transferred to the Coningsby wing 04.93 (still as 'FO'), flying with 5 Sqn that month before switching to 29 Sqn during 05.93, although flying with 56 [R] Sqn during 06.93. Had become 'AQ' by 11.94 before transferring back to 'BK'/29 Sqn. Again assigned to 'CK'/5 Sqn by 10.98 before returning to 56 [R] Sqn where it received an anniversary colour scheme. Sent to St Athan for storage on 18.10.00 and fuselage to EADS 01.01 for MLFP rebuild. Forward and rear fuselage remained stored at St Athan where it was noted in 09.92, 01.05 and 03.06. Finally disposed of for scrap on 09.03.06.
ZE340 AT025	First flew 22.10.87. Delivered to Coningsby 30.10.87. To 'AG'/229 OCU 12.87. Transferred to 111 Sqn (still as 'AG') 04.91. Reverted to 229 OCU 06.92 as 'AE'. Repainted in 56 [R] Sqn marks by 08.92. Received pseudo-AMI scheme with code 3612 for leasing handover on 04.07.95. To 5 Sqn on loan before reverting to its original 'AE'/56[R] Sqn markings in 01.01. Wfu and departed by road to the DCAE at Cosford on 07.09.01 now fitted with the tail from ZE758 coded 'GO'. Assigned maintenance serial 9298M and is still current.

ZE341 AS043	First flew 28.10.87. Delivered to Coningsby 06.11.87. To 'CF'/5 Sqn 12.87. To 'BC'/29 Sqn 08.88. Transferred to 111 Sqn 04.91 (still coded 'BC'), taking up the code 'HD' with the unit 09.91. To 1435 Flt as 'D' (Desperation), probably 01.94, returning to UK 09.96 and assigned as 'J'/111 Sqn. To 'AT'/56 [R] Sqn and then 'CL'/5 Sqn in 01.01. Recoded 'YU' in 05.02 and to 11 Sqn by 10.02. Took up code 'DF' and later loaned to FJWOEU. To 43 Sqn 05.05 receiving the code 'GO' by 12.05 until transfer to 111 Sqn at unit's demise. Assigned code 'HI' but still operated as 'GO' in 01.10.
ZE342 AS044	First flew 10.11.87. Delivered to Coningsby 20.11.87. To 'CG'/5 Sqn 01.88. Noted operating unmarked with 229 OCU during 04.88. To 'BK'/29 Sqn 06.88. To 111 Sqn 01.91 (still wearing 'BK' code); returned to 29 Sqn 02.91. Transferred to 23 Sqn (still as 'BK') 05.91, although had rejoined 111 Sqn by 06.91. To 'HE'/111 Sqn 09.91. Noted operating unmarked with 43 Sqn during 06.92. To Coningsby 07.92 (acted as airspare for Falklands deployment); operating unmarked with 29 Sqn during 08.92, switching to 23 Sqn by 10.92. By 11.92 flying (still unmarked) with 11 Sqn, although returned to 29 Sqn 12.92 (allocated the code 'BL'). To 'HW'/111 Sqn by 09.94 and recoded 'W' in 10.98 with revised toned-down unit markings. To 43 Sqn by 02.00 and 5 Sqn as 'HW' in 01.02. Following Sqn disbandment transferred to 'YS'/56 [R] Sqn in 08.02. Returned to Leuchars on loan by 10.02 with 111 Sqn and also operated with 43 Sqn. Assigned to 25 Sqn 05.03 receiving the code 'FG' by 03.06. Finally to 'HP'/111 Sqn in 03.08 and remains current.
ZE343 AT026	First flew 12.11.87. Delivered to Coningsby 20.11.87. To 'AN'/229 OCU 01.88. Recoded as 'AI' by 07.88. Operating with 11 Sqn during 08.91, although it had returned to 229 OCU (still coded 'AI') by 10.91. Stored St Athan by mid-'93 (centre fuselage damage). Received 'new' CF from donor aircraft ZD900 and following repair assigned to 'AA'/56 [R] Sqn. Recoded 'TI' by 05.01 and transferred to 'DZ'/11 Sqn in 05.05. To 111 Sqn by 11.05 but loaned to 56 [R] Sqn in 08.06. Placed in store at Leuchars 06.10.06 and flown to Leeming 09.03.09 for spares reclamation.
ZE728 AT027	First flew 14.10.87. Delivered to Boscombe Down 22.10.87 for tests with the A&AEE, returned to BAe Warton. Re-delivered to Coningsby 13.04.88, operating unmarked with 29 Sqn during 04.88, becoming 'BS' with the unit during 05.88 (noted however wearing the 11 Sqn code 'DH' on one side of the fin on 05.05.88, although this was soon replaced by 'BS'). Took part in Operation Golden Eagle between 21.8–25.10.88. To 'AA'/229 OCU 04.90. Recoded 'AN' with 229 OCU during 01.91. To 'AL'/56 [R] Sqn 03.93. Stored at St Athan by mid-'93 minus markings/code (centre fuselage damaged). Received donor CF from ZD903 and returned to service 12.05.97. Noted flying unmarked 10.97. Assigned to 'HX'/111 Sqn but later transferred to 'AH'/56 [R] Sqn before being recoded 'TH' and returning to 111 Sqn. To 25 Sqn by 11.02 and coded 'FA' by 12.06 later altered to 'FZ'. Reassigned to 111 Sqn 04.08 and allocated the code 'HZ' but never carried. Transferred to 43 Sqn 06.08 until wfu and taken by road to Leeming 21.04.09 for RTP. Later shipped to scrap metal dealer in Seaham for final disposal only for the hulk to be bought by the Commission for the Cultural Olympiad in the North East for artist Fiona Banner to turn into a giant bell.

ZE729 AS045	First Flew 19.11.87. Delivered to Coningsby 21.12.87. Operating with F3OEU 01.88. Noted operating unmarked with 25 Sqn during 07.89. To 23 Sqn as 'EC' 08.89. Loaned to 25 Sqn, 11.89. Switched to 43 Sqn (still as 'EC') 30.08.90. To 'CD'/5 Sqn 10.90. Reverted to 'EC'/23 Sqn by 01.91, although transferred to 29 Sqn as 'BF' 06.91. Stored St Athan by mid-'93 minus markings/code (damaged fuselage only).Received donor CF from ZD933 and repaired at Warton in 02.96. Assigned to 56 [R] Sqn as 'AQ' 09.96 then to 'CF'/5 Sqn by 01.98 but suffered a major in-flight generator failure en route from Gioia del Colle to Akrotiri and had to be returned by road on 06.10.98. Assigned to 11 Sqn but transferred to 1435 Flt 25.09.99 on temporary loan to participate in an airshow at Rio de Janeiro. Returned to the UK 05.10.99 only to be shipped out to the Falkland Islands, this time by Antonov An-124 on 17.01.00. It returned this time to St Athan by C-17 on 16.01.02. Assigned to 'YR'/11 Sqn by 10.02 but recoded 'DH' in 06.04. Reported wfu and undergoing spares recovery at Leeming in 08.05.
ZE730 AS046	First flew 25.11.87. Delivered to Coningsby 21.12.87. To F3OEU 01.88. Flown to Leeming 29.06.89, and with 11 Sqn as 'DF' 08.89. Noted operating with 111 Sqn 09.90, although it had lost its marks/code by 01.91. To 'CD'/5 Sqn 02.91, although was operating as such with 11 Sqn during 03.91. To 111 Sqn (still coded 'CD') 04.91. Noted unmarked with 43 Sqn by 02.92. Took part in the Kuwait Liberation 1st Anniversary Flypast between 22–27.02.92. To 'GL'/43 Sqn 06.93. Leased to AMI as MM7204/3605. Returned to UK at end of lease period 25.02.04 for spares reclamation at St Athan. Fuselage dumped 03.05 and noted at various times up until 01.07. Finally disposed of as scrap 04.10.97 to M. Williams & Son, Hitchin.
ZE731 AS047	First flew 03.12.87. Delivered to Coningsby 21.12.87. Operating with the F3OEU 01.88. Noted operating unmarked with 25 Sqn 06–09.89. To 111 Sqn (still unmarked) on 30.08.90. To 'CH'/5 Sqn 02.91, although rejoined 111 Sqn by 04.91 (still as 'CH'). Operated with both 43 and 111 Sqns between 04–07.91, eventually remaining on strength with the latter. By 02.92 had joined 43 Sqn (unmarked). To 'GK'/43 Sqn 09.92. Recoded 'GF' and given anniversary colour scheme of black spine and fin inscribed with '1916–1996 80th Anniversary' legend in 02.96. To 5 Sqn then 56 [R] Sqn in 09.01 and coded 'YP' by 05.02. To 25 Sqn by 06.02 and with 111 Sqn by deployed to Dhahran for the second Gulf campaign. On return transferred to 43 Sqn in 04.03 and eventually coded 'GP'. Placed in store at Leuchars in 09.09 and flown to Leeming for spares reclamation on 24.11.09.

Then the Tornado Operational Evaluation Unit (TOEU), ZE730, sporting the units stylised motif on the fin, is seen landing at RAF Coningsby during 1988. Its tenure with the unit was quite brief before transfer to No.XI Squadron. Subsequently it became part of the AMI lease programme and following its period of use in Italy it was scrapped.

ZE732 AS048	First flew 17.12.87. Delivered to Coningsby 08.01.88, becoming 'CH'/5 Sqn 02.88. Deployed to Dhahran 11.08.90 as part of 5 [C] Sqn. To 43 Sqn (still coded 'CH') by late 09.90. Operating unmarked with 43 and 111 Sqns during 04.91, eventually staying with 111 Sqn during 07.91 until it switched to 43 Sqn by 02.92. Took part in the Kuwait Liberation 1st Anniversary Flypast held over 22–27.02.92. To 'GI'/43 Sqn 11.92. Transferred to 'AS'/56 [R] Sqn by 02.95 but was being operated by 29 Sqn when it crashed 30 nautical miles NE of Flamborough Head on 15.06.98.
ZE733 AS049	First flew 11.12.87. Delivered to Coningsby 08.01.88, becoming 'CI'/5 Sqn 02.88. To 'BF'/29 Sqn by 12.88. To 'FH'/25 Sqn 09.89. To 43 Sqn on 30.08.90, and had lost its marks/code by the end of 09.90. Returned to 5 Sqn by 01.91. To 'CL'/5 Sqn late 02.91, but switched to 11 Sqn (still as 'CL') during 03.91. Transferred to 111 Sqn 04.91 (again still wearing the 'CL' code). To 'GE'/43 Sqn 08.91. Lost on 30.10.95 following a mid-air collision with ZE210.
ZE734 AS050	First flew 07.01.88. Delivered to Coningsby 25.01.88, becoming 'CJ'/5 Sqn 02.88. Deployed to Dhahran 11.08.90 as part of 5 [C] Sqn. To 25 Sqn by 02.91 (still coded 'CJ'), although returned to 5 Sqn 04.91; recoded 'CX' with the unit 03.92. To 11 Sqn 10.92 (still coded 'CX'), reverting to 5 Sqn early 93. Transferred to 43 Sqn (still as 'CX') 10.93. but recoded 'GB' by 01.94. Loaned to 25 Sqn and recoded 'YO' in late 02. To 'DA'/11 Sqn 09.01.04 before returning to 43 Sqn. Transferred to 111 Sqn 02.07 and received 90th nniversary special scheme and the code 'JU', which it retains today.
ZE735 AT028	First flew 13.01.88. Delivered to Coningsby 02.02.88, becoming 'CT'/5 Sqn 03.88. To 'FE'/25 Sqn 07.89. Flown to Coningsby 24.11.89, and operating unmarked with 229 OCU by 12.89. To 'AL' with that unit during 02.90. Noted in the Coningsby ASF 05.93 with CAT 3 damage following an engine fire whilst in Cyprus. Returned to service by 09.95 with 56 [R] Sqn and recoded 'TG' by 02.03. Received unit's 90th Anniversary special scheme 22.05.06 which it retained until flown to Leeming 12.11.08 for spares reclamation.
ZE736 AS051	First flew 20.01.88. Delivered to Coningsby 02.02.88, becoming 'CK'/5 Sqn the same month. Flew to Dhahran 11.08.90 as part of 5 [C] Sqn. Operated unmarked with 111 Sqn 04.91, becoming 'HA' with the unit 07.91. Noted flying with 25 Sqn (still as 'HA') 05.92, although it had returned to 111 Sqn by 08.92. Stored St Athan by mid-'93 (centre fuselage damaged). Received 'new' CF from donor aircraft ZD937 and repaired at Warton 02.96. Issued to 56 [R] Sqn as 'AB' but code not taken up and was subsequently allocated 'AX'. To 111 Sqn becoming 'K' by 02.01. Recoded 'YN' before assigned to 1435 Flt on 10.01.02 and was flown to the Falkland Islands by C-17. Had returned to the UK by 06.04 where it became 'HC'/111 Sqn. To 'WB'/56 [R] Sqn in special marks 07.05. Returned to 1435 Flt 08.06 as 'F' (Faith) returning 09.08 to Leeming for spares reclamation.
ZE737 AS052	First flew 29.01.88. Delivered to Coningsby 11.02.88, becoming 'CE'/5 Sqn the same month. Noted operating with 43 Sqn (still as 'CE') during 11.90. Noted operating at Leeming 16.01.91 coded 'K'/no marks. Arrived back in the UK (Leuchars) 13.03.91 with 43 [C] Sqn (believed to have deployed to Dhahran during 02.91). Operating as 'K' with 25 Sqn during 04.91. To 'FF'/25 Sqn by the following month and still current 11.96. With 111 Sqn in 10.02 and coded 'YM' when deployed to Dhahran for the second Gulf campaign. Received the name 'Stanford Tuck' and the number 28 alongside artwork depicting four Ace playing cards on the starboard side of nose wheel door. It received artwork on the port side depicting the 'Roger the Dodger' cartoon character with the inscription 'The Dodger'. Transferred to 43 Sqn and then to 25 Sqn on loan in 04.05. Returned to 43 Sqn by 07.05 and allocated the code 'GK' and was so coded in 03.06. Assigned to the BAE Systems test fleet 25.04.06 but retired in 2008 and taken by road from Warton to Shawbury for storage 19.11.08. Still current 10.10.
ZE755 AS053	First flew 05.02.88. Delivered 24.02.88, becoming 'CG' with 5 Sqn 03.88; operating unmarked with 111 Sqn during 04.91. although it had transferred to 43 Sqn later the same month. To 'GB'/43 Sqn 06.91. Recoded 'GJ' by 04.97 when deployed with 111 Sqn to Butterworth for Exercise Flying Fish but placed into short term store at St Athan by 09.00. Re-assigned as 'YL'/111 Sqn in 06.02 transferring to 25 Sqn in 10.03 but operated uncoded in 07.05. Loaned to Qinetiq 18.01.06 but flown to Leeming for RTP on 27.03.08.
ZE756 AS054	First flew 18.02.88. To 'CD'/5 Sqn 03.88; returned to Warton by 06.88 to join the trials fleet, being used as the Foxhunter radar development a/c (with A&AEE during 08.89). Delivered to Coningsby 04.12.91 to join the F3OEU for further radar trials. Flown to St Athan 31.07.00 for storage where it remained until 04.10.07 when it was disposed of as scrap to M. Williams & Son, Hitchin.
ZE757 AS055	First flew 19.02.88. Noted at BAe Warton 08.88 in use with the Saudi Support Unit. Flying with 111 Sqn by 04.91 (unmarked). To 'GF'/43 Sqn 06.91, taking up 75th anniversary marks by 09.91. Flew in the Kuwait Liberation 1st Anniversary Flypast between 22–27.02.92. Loaned to 23 Sqn 05.92. Recoded as 'GA' 43 Sqn during 10.93, 'GF' in 09.94 and 'GK' in 02.96. To 'AR'/56 [R] Sqn by 02.99 before transfer to 11 Sqn where by 07.01 it had received the code 'YJ'. To 25 Sqn so coded in 12.01 before receiving the code 'FI' in 10.03. To 43 Sqn 08.06 and placed in store at Leuchars 05.09. Flown to Leeming for spares reclamation during 07.09.
ZE758 AS056	First flew 19.02.88. Delivered to Coningsby 09.03.88, becoming 'CB'/5 Sqn that month. Deployed as part of 5 [C] Sqn to Dhahran 11.08.90 (returned to the UK on 23.09.90 – the last aircraft to leave Dhahran from the original deployment). To 29 Sqn by 04.91 as 'BH'. Unmarked at Coningsby during 07.92, prior to deploying to the Falkland Islands to join 1435 Flt as 'C' on 08.07.92 (named 'Charity'), returning in 01.94 to 56 [R] Sqn. Transferred to 'HV'/111 Sqn by 09.94 before passing onto 'CH'/5 Sqn. Returned to 56 Sqn as 'AU' by 05.98 but this was short-lived before reassignment to 43 Sqn in 09.98 where it was allocated the code 'GO'. Following recoding to 'YI' it passed to 5 Sqn by 09.01 and deployed to Dhahran with 111 Sqn for the second Gulf campaign. Upon return assigned to 11 Sqn and was recoded with the unit in 06.04 as 'DO'. Served with 111 Sqn in 10.05 and 25 Sqn in 10.06, finally returning to 111 Sqn in 06.07 where it was allocated the code 'HD'. Flown to Leeming 16.04.09 for spares reclamation.

ZE759 AT029	First flew 26.02.88. Delivered to Coningsby 09.03.88, becoming 'BT'/29 Sqn that month. Took part in Operation 'Golden Eagle' between 21.08–25.10.88. To 'AN'/229 OCU during 11.88. To 'FC'/25 Sqn 07.89. To 43 Sqn (still as 'FC'/25 Sqn marks) on 30.08.90. To 'CI'/5 Sqn 10.90. To 26 Sqn by 02.91 (wore full unit marks despite retaining the 'CI' code), eventually taking up the 'FC' code once again during 03.91. To 'A3'/229 OCU by 11.91. To 'AG'/229 OCU (no marks) 03.92. Stored St Athan minus marks/code by mid-'93 (damaged fuselage only). Received CF from donor aircraft ZD904 and repaired at Warton in 02.96. However, lost on a test flight from the company's airfield on 28.09.96 crashing into the sea off Blackpool following a missed approach – BAE Systems crew ejecting safely.
ZE760 AS057	First flew 10.03.88. Delivered to Coningsby 28.03.88, becoming 'CF' with 5 Sqn 04.88. Flying with 229 OCU (still as 'CF') during 02.90, taking up the code 'AP' late 02.90 (5 Sqn marks were retained for a short time). Carried out a wheels-up landing at Coningsby on 07.06.90 (returned to service by early 1991, with a small cartoon of a Tornado being lifted by a cradle on the fin). Transferred to 43 Sqn (still coded 'AP') by 06.92. To 'GP'/43 Sqn 10.92. Assigned to AMI lease programme as MM7206/3607. Upon expiry of lease period returned to Coningsby where it has been preserved as the gate guardian.

ZE761 AS058	First flew 14.03.88. Delivered to Leeming 28.03.88 for use as a maintenance trainer. To Coningsby 22.04.88 becoming 'CC'/5 Sqn 05.88. Recoded as 'CB' with the unit by 10.90. Loaned to the Leeming Wing 11.93 but back at Coningsby as 'AP'/56 [R] Sqn by 09.94. Assigned to the AMI lease programme as MM7203/3602 and returned to St Athan on 04.08.03 at end of period. Became part of BAE Systems test fleet on 08.12.03 until returned to St Athan for storage in 01.07.
ZE762 AS059	First flew 11.03.88. Delivered to Coningsby 30.03.88, and became 'CA' with 5 Sqn during 04.88. Deployed to RMAFB Butterworth during 03.90 as part of Exercise IADS 90. Deployed to Dhahran 11.08.90 with 5 [C] Sqn. Noted operating with 25 Sqn (still as 'CA') during 02.91. To 'CD'/5 Sqn by 06.91. To 'AX'/229 OCU 11.91. Transferred to 29 Sqn as 'BB' 03.92. Noted unmarked at Coningsby late 06.92 (acted as groundspare for 1435 Flt deployment on 07.07.92). Operating with 29 Sqn (unmarked) during 08.92, taking up the 'BB' code once again by 12.92. To 43 Sqn (unmarked) 03.93, being coded 'GM' with the unit by 05.93. Assigned to AMI lease programme as MM7207/3620 but later recoded 3627. Returned to St Athan 31.03.04 at end of lease period and remained stored until 2005 when it entered the spares reclamation programme. Airframe dumped by 04.05 finally departing for scrapping 27.10.05.
ZE763 AS060	First flew 25.03.88. Delivered to Coningsby 22.04.88, becoming 'CD'/5 Sqn 05.88. Loaned to 43 Sqn 11.90 (still as 'CD'). Transferred to Leeming by 09.01.91, and in use with 11 Sqn coded 'A' by 16.01.91. Returned to the UK (Coningsby) 13.03.91 coded 'BA'/29 Sqn, when elements of that unit arrived back from the Gulf as part of 43 [C] Sqn. Did not deploy to the Gulf theatre, being marked with 29 Sqn's insignia for the arrival celebrations. In use with the F3OEU 05.91 (still coded 'BA'). Transferred to 23 Sqn 10.91, although back in use with 29 Sqn by 01.92. Took part in Exercise Red Flag 93/1 during 10–11.92, returning to the UK with 11 Sqn (still marked as 'BA'/29 Sqn). To 'DG'/11 Sqn 04.93 remaining with unit until at least 06.05 during which period it trialled the SEAD fit with ALARM missiles. To 25 Sqn by 10.05 and recoded 'FJ' in 03.06. Re-assigned to 43 Sqn in 03.08 where it was allocated the code 'GD' but thought not to have carried same. Re-assigned to 111 Sqn following disbandment of 43 Sqn and allocated the code 'HD'. Current 01.10.
ZE764 AS061	First flew 25.03.88. Delivered to Coningsby 26.04.88. To 'DH'/11 Sqn 05.88. Flown to Leeming 01.07.88, and special marks (for the squadron CO) were applied during early 09.88 (black fin/spine; codes and serials in gold). Transferred to 111 Sqn on 30.08.90, becoming 'HC' with the unit late 09.90. At Leeming 09.01.91 unmarked, and reportedly took up the code 'DH' once again by mid-01.91. Deployed to Dhahran during 02.91, joining 43 [C] Sqn as 'I'. Returned to UK (Leuchars) 13.03.91. Operating as 'I' with 11 Sqn during 04.91, becoming 'DH' once again by 06.91. Loaned to 111 Sqn where it was recoded 'YD' in 05.02. Transferred as 'FK'/25 Sqn 01.06 and then 'GL'/43 Sqn in 02.08. At demise of 43 Sqn passed to 111 Sqn as 'HK' and current 01.10.

Set against the familiar mountain backdrop of Nellis AFB, Nevada, are six Tornado F.3 stage 1+ aircraft deployed for Exercise Red Flag 93/1. Nearest the camera is ZE763/DA, then ZE887/DJ, ZE907/EN, ZE961/FD, ZE982/DM and ZE962/FJ. At the time the deployment was being crewed by No.5 Squadron from RAF Coningsby.

ZE785 AS062	First flew 30.03.88. Delivered to Coningsby 06.05.88. To 'DA'/11 Sqn 05.88. Flown to Leeming 01.07.88. Noted back at Coningsby during 12.89, and seen as 'AX'/229 OCU 01.90. Recoded as 'AO' 04.90. Special 65 [R] Sqn 75th anniversary marks applied 12.90 for celebrations the following year (with the unit's lion emblem replacing the OCU sword/torch insignia on the fin, together with the inscription '75 YEARS' flanked by smaller '1916' and '1991' legends. A white arrowhead edged in red on the leading edges was applied to the top of the fin, in which was the code 'AO'. These marks were altered to commemorate 65 Sqn's 76th anniversary in 07.92). Repainted in 56 [R] Sqn marks by 10.92 (still coded 'AO'). Believed to have been flown to St Athan for attention 06.93. Returned to 'AT'/56 [R] Sqn 03.94 but passed to F3OEU in 08.01 as 'YJ'. Remained with unit through transition to FJWOEU and 41 [R] Sqn changes before joining 111 Sqn in 02.08 where it was assigned the code 'HS'. Received commemorative 90th anniversary markings in 06.08 but flown to Leeming 12.05.09 for spares reclamation.
ZE786 AT030	First flew 31.03.88. Delivered to Coningsby 20.05.88. To 'DT'/11 Sqn 06.88, and flown to Leeming on 06.07.88. Loaned to 111 Sqn during 09.90. To 'FM'/25 Sqn 02.91, although switched to 5 Sqn (still as 'FM') by 04.91. To 'CF'/5 Sqn 07.91. Recoded as 'CT' 11.91. Stored St Athan unmarked mid-'93 (damaged fuselage only). Received CF from donor aircraft ZD934 and repaired at Warton 02.96. Became 'AG'/56 [R] Sqn in 06.96 and 'AN' in 09.99. Recoded 'TF' at some point pre-10.03, it was transferred to 43 Sqn by 03.07 and finally dispatched to Leeming in 12.08 for RTP.
ZE787 AS063	First flew 11.04.88. Delivered to Coningsby 13.05.88. To 'DB'/11 Sqn 06.88, and flew to Leeming 01.07.88. Operating with 23 Sqn 01.91 (still coded 'DB'). To 111 Sqn 02.91 (still as 'DB'). To 'AV'/229 OCU 03.91. Noted operating with 11 Sqn 05.92 (still as 'AV'). To 'EX'/23 Sqn 08.92. To 111 Sqn (still as 'EH') 02.93, becoming 'HM' 06.93. Assigned to AMI lease programme as MM7205/3606 it returned to RAF charge at St Athan 07.06.04 where it was placed into store and finally reclaimed for spares. It was disposed of to scrap 18.09.07 to M. Williams & Son, Hitchin.
ZE788 AS064	First flew 18.04.88. Delivered to Coningsby 14.06.88. To 'DC'/11Sqn 06.88, and flown to Leeming during 07.88. Noted operating unmarked with 111 Sqn 10.90. To 'S' by 21.01.91 (operated by 11 Sqn). To 25 Sqn (still as 'S') 03.91, becoming 'FH' with the unit by 06.91. To 'DF'/11 Sqn 01.93. Loaned to 5 Sqn 06.09.93–11.93. Returned to 25 Sqn before being assigned to the F3OEU or AWC as it had become in 09.96 although noted operating uncoded but in 5 Sqn markings during 07.99. Recoded 'YA' it was with 111 Sqn in 10.02. Following CAT 3 damage it was re-issued to 43 Sqn in 02.04 still as 'YA' and coded 'GL' in 08.04. Loaned to BAE Systems as part of its test fleet in 08.05, it was returned to RAF charge with 111 Sqn on 15.04.08 becoming 'HV'. Received special 90th anniversary markings in 06.08; it later reverted to original scheme by 07.09. Wfu a month later and sent to Leeming for RTP.

ZE789 AS065	First flew 25.04.88. Delivered to Coningsby 06.06.88. To 'DD'/11 Sqn 07.88. To 'FI'/25 Sqn 07.90. Flown to Leuchars for 43 Sqn on 30.08.90 (still as 'FI'/25 Sqn marks), and remained in use there with both 43 and 111 Sqns up until 04.91. Switched to 229 OCU 06.91 (still wearing 'FI'/25 Sqn marks), becoming 'AW' with the unit by 07.91. Stored St Athan unmarked by mid-'93 (damaged fuselage only). Re-issued to 56 [R] Sqn as 'AW' by 07.91 it was to receive the special display scheme of red fin and spine for the 1994 display season. It was lost in a accident on 10.03.95 when it crashed into the North Sea off Spurn Head.
ZE790 AS066	First flew 06.05.88. Delivered to Coningsby 16.06.88, and became 'DE'/11 Sqn 07.88. Switched to 111 Sqn 01.91 (still as 'DE'), and operated with 43 Sqn 03/04.91 before returning to 111 Sqn. To 'HC'/111 Sqn 08.91. Noted unmarked at Coningsby early 07.92, arriving at Mount Pleasant 08.07.92 for 1435 Flt, coded 'D' and named 'Desperation'. Returned in 01.94 to 56 [R] Sqn taking up the code 'AW' by 05.94 and 'AO' in 06.95. Passed to 11 Sqn on loan by 01.96 before being assigned as 'GD'/43 Sqn a month later. Recoded 'VU' in 02.96 but was unmarked when it deployed with 111 Sqn to Butterworth for Exercise Flying Fish in 04.97. Reverted to 'GD' by 03.01. It was back with 11 Sqn by 06.02 becoming 'YU' and had received the code 'DK' by 07.04. Passed to 111 Sqn as 'HC' in 10.05, it was to remain with the unit until stored at Leuchars in 07.09. Flown to Leeming 09.09.09 for spares reclamation.
ZE791 AS067	First flew 13.05.88. Handed over to the RAF on 22.06.88 as the 100th production ADV variant (delivered to Coningsby the same day). To 'DF'/11 Sqn 07.88, and was flown to Leeming on 28.07.88. To 'FF'/25 Sqn 10.89. Transferred to 229 OCU (still as 'FF'/25 Sqn marks) 07.91, becoming 'A9' with the unit 08.91. Noted as 'A9'/56 [R] Sqn in 06.93 but back with 25 Sqn as 'FP' and sporting revised Sqn marks in 10.94. To 'HY'/111 Sqn 04.96 before passing to 5 Sqn in 03.98 and receiving the code 'CD' a month later. Aircraft received special marks by 06.98 but had moved to Leuchars and 111 Sqn in 11.98. Coded 'N' initially, it later became 'XY' by 05.01. With 43 Sqn in 10.02 but loaned to 11 Sqn in 05.04. Back with 111 Sqn as 'HF' with whom it is current 01.10.
ZE792 AS068	First flew 27.05.88. Delivered to Coningsby 12.07.88. To 'DG'/11 Sqn late 07.88. Flown to Leuchars 30.08.90 for 111 Sqn, losing its marks/code during 09.90. Switched to 5 Sqn 01.91 (still unmarked), becoming 'CE' the following month. To 111 Sqn (as 'CE') 04.91. To 43 Sqn as 'GJ' 03.92, although it had lost all markings during 06.92. Noted unmarked at Coningsby early 07.92 acting as airspare for the Falklands deployment over 07–08.07.92. To 'CU'/5 Sqn 08.92. Returned once again to 111 Sqn 02.93, retaining the 'CU' code for a short while. Then operated unmarked, although the code 'HL' was believed allocated. Allocated to the AMI lease programme, it became MM7211/3616. Returned to RAF charge at end of lease period 24.10.03 at St Athan and entered the spares reclamation programme in 12.04. Eventually scrapped and dispatched to Beaver Metals, Water Orton, for disposal 11.01.05.

ZE793 AT031	First flew 20.05.88. Noted operating with BAe 06.88. Delivered to Coningsby 21.07.88, to 11 Sqn (unmarked) 08.88, becoming 'DZ' later that month. To 'AK'/229 OCU 02.90. Repainted in 56 [R] Sqn marks 08.92 (still as 'AK'). Noted 04.93 at St Athan in store with fuselage damage. Received 'new' CF from donor aircraft ZD935 and returned to service at Coningsby on 26.03.97. Became 'AI'/56 [R] Sqn it was loaned to 5 Sqn in 08.01 where it was recoded 'TE'. To 43 Sqn by 10.02 and 25 Sqn 03.04 before returning to 56 [R] Sqn a month later. Re-assigned permanently as 'FY'/25 Sqn 04.05, it passed into store at Leuchars before being returned to Leeming 05.03.09 for spares reclamation.
ZE794 AS069	First flew 03.06.88. Delivered to Coningsby 29.06.88, although it had repositioned to Leeming by late 08.88. To 'DI'/11Sqn 09.88. To 'FD'/25 Sqn 07.89. Transferred to 43 Sqn 09.90 (uncoded by the end of that month). Noted operating unmarked with 25 Sqn 01.91, 111 Sqn 02.91, and then back to 25 Sqn during 03.91. To Coningsby during 04.91. Operated with 29 Sqn for a short while before joining 229 OCU as 'A4' by 09.91. To 111 Sqn (still as 'A4') 04.92. To 'HQ'/111 Sqn 08.93. Recoded 'A' with revised Sqn markings. Passed to 5 Sqn it was loaned to DERA in 04.01 but back with Sqn in 05.01. A short period with 11 Sqn followed before transferring to 43 Sqn in 12.02. Coded 'XW' it next transferred to 25 Sqn by 05.03 and apart from a short loan period with 56 [R] Sqn in 08.06 remained with unit until transfer to 43 Sqn in 01.08 by which time it had been coded 'FL'. Assigned to Qinetiq 03.08 and current 01.10.
ZE808 AS070	First flew 10.06.88. Delivered to Coningsby 29.07.88. To 'DJ'/11 Sqn 08.88. To 43 Sqn (still as 'DJ'/11 Sqn marks) by 04.09.90, but became 'GF'/43 Sqn by 14.09.90. Coded 'C' at Leeming 28.01.91. Operating with 11 Sqn (still as 'C'/no marks) during 03.91. To 'FA'/25 Sqn 05.91; loaned to 111 Sqn 03.92 for Exercise Distant Frontier 92 in Alaska on 06.04.92; returned to 25 Sqn by 05.92. First aircraft to receive revised squadron markings of silver/black nose-bars with 'XXV' on a silver band on the fin, first noted 09.94. With 11 Sqn when right-hand undercarriage leg collapsed on landing at Leeming on 16.03.00. By road to St Athan but returned to 25 Sqn 22.08.01 unmarked. Loaned to BAE Systems test fleet 13.01.05 until re-assigned to 111 Sqn 15.05.08 as 'HJ'. To Leuchars store 05.09 until flown to Leeming for RTP 30.07.09.
ZE809 AS071	First flew 23.06.88; Delivered to Leeming 05.08.88, joining 23 Sqn as 'EZ' by 09.88. Adopted special 23 Sqn marks during 05.90 for the unit's 75th anniversary that year (consisting of blue/red fin with enlarged squadron emblem, and the titling '23 SQUADRON – 75TH ANNIVERSARY 1 SEPTEMBER 1990' along the spine). To 'CE'/5 Sqn 07.91. Switched to 111 Sqn 04.92 (still as 'CE'). To 'HP'/111Sqn 06.92. Took part in the static display for the Royal Review at Marham 01.04.93. Lost 60 nautical miles east of Newcastle 07.06.94 when being operated by 11 Sqn.
ZE810 AS072	First flew 30.06.88. Delivered to Leeming 15.08.88, becoming 'EN'/23 Sqn during 09.88. Unmarked with 23 Sqn 07-08.89, reverting to 'EN' afterwards. Operating with 29 Sqn (still as 'EN') 04.91. To 'A8'/229 OCU 08.91. Noted unmarked at Coningsby early 07.92, acting as ground spare for the re-equipment of 1435 Flt over 07–08.07.92. Unmarked with 56 [R] Sqn from 08.92, finally becoming 'AT'/full marks with the unit during 06.93. With 111 Sqn as 'HP' by 12.94 but later recoded 'P'. With 43 Sqn still coded 'HP' in 07.98. On loan to DERA 02.01 but returned to 43 Sqn by 05.01 later becoming code 'XU'. Used by both 111 Sqn and 43 Sqn throughout 2002 until assigned permanently to 43 Sqn in 10.04. Initially allocated the code 'GM' but not carried then may have become 'GG' after 07.06. To Leuchars store 07.09 and flown to Leeming for RTP 10.08.09.
ZE811 AS073	First flew 15.07.88; Delivered to Leeming 19.08.88, becoming 'DK'/11 Sqn by 12.88. To 'DI'/11 Sqn 07.89, and eventually wore the improvised serial of 'ZE8XI' by 06.90. To 111 Sqn 30.08.90 (still as 'ZE8XI'/DI). Devoid of code/marks by 04.91 but still marked as 'ZE8XI' during 07.91. To 'HB'/111 Sqn 08.91, with the serial in normal style. To 56 [R] Sqn 08.95 as 'A8' but assigned to AMI loan programme as MM7208/3611. Recoded 3622 and returned to St Athan at end of lease period on 05.12.03. Spares recovered during 2004 and noted dumped on 26.10.04. Sold for scrap to Williams Scrap Yard, Hitchin, departing St Athan 16.11.04.
ZE812 AS074	First flew 22.07.88. Delivered to Leeming 30.08.88, becoming 'EA'/23 Sqn during 09.88. Passed to 111 Sqn (still as 'EA') 04.91. To 229 OCU (again still coded 'EA') 06.91, becoming 'AY'/229 OCU 08.91. Noted unmarked at Coningsby early 07.92, deploying to the Falkland Islands 07-08.07.92 to join 1435 Flt as 'F' (named 'Faith'). Returned to UK by 06.95 joining BAE Systems test fleet but to ASF Coningsby by 08.96 and assigned as 'CW'/5 Sqn. At St Athan 27.09.96 to 19.11.96 and flown to Warton 02.12.96. With 111 Sqn by 06.98 until flown to Falkland Islands for 1435 Flt 23.09.98. Later with 5 Sqn as 'CW' and then 56 [R] Sqn as 'AV' by 11.00. Recoded 'XR' and assigned to 111 Sqn by 11.01. With 25 Sqn by 06.02 and back with 56 [R] Sqn by 09.02. Wfu at St Athan and sold to Metal & Waste for scrapping 03.06.
ZE830 AT032	First flew 12.08.88. Delivered to Leeming 19.09.88. Noted flying unmarked during 11.88, becoming 'ET'/23 Sqn later that month. To 43 Sqn (still as 'ET'/23 Sqn marks) on 30.08.90, and noted unmarked with 111 Sqn 01.91, back to 43 Sqn by 04.91. To 'GD'/43 Sqn 06.91. With 111 Sqn as 'HU' by 11.95 but loaned to F3OEU when it was lost over the North Sea on 17.11.99 following an in-flight fire. Wreck salvaged and returned to Coningsby and stored in an ISO container. Remains put out for tender (No.3054) as Lot 11W for scrap 24.01.02.
ZE831 AS075	First flew 05.08.88. Delivered to Leeming 04.10.88, becoming 'EW'/23 Sqn during 11.88. To 111 Sqn (as 'EW') 01.91, although transferred to 43 Sqn by 04.91. To 'HJ'/111 Sqn 09.91. To 'GG'/43 Sqn 10.93. To 1435 Flt 08.96 as airspare returning to Coningsby 28.09.96 and to 56 [R] Sqn still as '43/GG'. Unmarked when it deployed to Butterworth as part of Exercise Flying Fish in 04.97. Recoded 'XQ' and with 25 Sqn 11.02. Noted with 111 Sqn but still 25 Sqn marks. Allocated code 'FM' in 08.06 and then 'AW' with 56 [R] Sqn 09.06. Returned to 43 Sqn as 'GN' 05.08 until placed in store at Leuchars in 07.09. To Leeming for RTP 07.07.09.

ZE832 AS076	First flew 19.08.88. Delivered to Leeming 07.09.88, and became 'EB'/23 Sqn later that month. To 111 Sqn during 09.90 (still as 'EB'/23 Sqn marks), operating unmarked with 23 Sqn during 01.91, but reverted to 111 Sqn by 03.91. To 43 Sqn (still unmarked) 04.91. To 'A7'/229 OCU 08.91. Loaned to F3OEU during 06–07.92. Assigned to AMI loan programme as MM7202/3612 until returned to St Athan at end of lease on 26.04.03. Re-issued to 56 [R] Sqn as 'XP' 24.09.03 until wfu for spares recovery in 07.05.
ZE833 AS077	First flew 26.08.88. Delivered to Leeming 07.10.88. To 'EC'/23 Sqn 11.88. W/o 21.07.89 when it crashed into the sea 30 nautical miles north-east of Newcastle-upon-Tyne.
ZE834 AS078	First flew 16.09.88. Delivered to Leeming 01.11.88, became 'ED'/23 Sqn during that month. Received CAT 4 damage 05.07.89 whilst attending APC at Akrotiri when the nose-wheel collapsed on landing. Roaded back to Leeming 09.10.89 and underwent rebuild . Re-assigned to 25 Sqn and allocated the code 'FX'. To 'GM'/43 Sqn by 02.96 and to 1435 Flt as 'H' ('Hope') in 05.97. Returned to 5 Sqn (still in 1435 marks) 09.98 and allocated the code 'CX' in 01.99. Noted wearing new style unit markings with the traditional Maple Leaf having been replaced by a yellow number '5'. Recoded 'XO' in 05.01 and back to 1435 Flt 23.05.01. Returned to UK and with 111 Sqn as 'HD' in 08.05. Again with 1435 Flt on 17.04.07 as 'D' ('Desperation') but returned to UK 16.10.09. Allocated to 111 Sqn as 'HA' whom it remains current.
ZE835 AS079	First flew 21.09.88. Delivered to Leeming 31.10.88, becoming 'EE'/23 Sqn during 11.88. To 43 Sqn on 30.08.90 (still as 'EE'/23 Sqn marks). Reportedly to 'CE'/5 Sqn 10.90 (code possibly only allocated and not worn). Returned to 23 Sqn as 'EE' 01.91, although transferred to 111 Sqn (still as 'EE') later that month. To 'HK'/111 Sqn 07.92. Allocated to the AMI loan programme becoming MM7209/3613. Returned to St Athan at end of lease period in 10.04 and noted in store in 03.05. Stripped for spares, the fuselage was noted dumped in 08.05 and sold to M. Williams & Sons, Hitchin for scrapping 04.10.07.
ZE836 AS080	First flew 23.09.88. Delivered to Leeming 22.11.88. To 'EF'/23 Sqn during 12.88. To 'CH'/5 Sqn 06.91. To 'AS'/229 OCU 01.92. Remained with unit and re-assigned as 56 Sqn 'AY' by 04.95 but allocated to AMI loan programme becoming MM7210/3614. Retained in Italy at end of lease and currently preserved at Vigna di Valle.
ZE837 AT033	First flew 30.09.88. Delivered to Leeming during 22.11.88. To 'EQ'/23 Sqn during 12.88. Noted operating unmarked with 25 Sqn 11.89. To 'FL'/25 Sqn 07.90. Switched to 43 Sqn on 28.08.90, and unmarked during late 09.90. To 'CF'/5 Sqn 03.91. Reverted to 111 Sqn (still coded 'CF') 04.91, although passed to 43 Sqn later that month. To 'GH'/43 Sqn 09.91. To 'HY'/111 Sqn 09.92. To 'GI'/43 Sqn 05.95 and assigned to AMI loan programme becoming MM55057/3603. Returned to St Athan in 2003 at end of lease and re-assigned to 56 [R] Sqn as 'TD' 02.09.03. Wfu Leuchars 11.05 and fuselage noted stored St Athan 01.07.

ZE838 AS081	First flew 09.11.88. Delivered to Leeming 12.01.89. To 'FA'/25 Sqn 07.89. Special marks applied for unit's 75th anniversary during 05.90 (silver band, edged in black, applied to fin/spine, with the unit's crest surmounted on the fin plus '1915' and '1990' placed either side of the badge; eight of the squadron's battle honour 'scrolls' were carried on the nose). Noted operating with 111 Sqn 01.91 (as 'FA'/25 Sqn marks). To 'BB'/29 Sqn 07.91. To 'A3'/229 OCU 03.92. Transferred to 111 Sqn (still coded 'A3') 05.92. To 'HO'/111 Sqn 06.92. To 'GH'/43 Sqn. Re-assigned to 25 Sqn and allocated the code 'FE' in 06.95 but never carried. Returned to 43 Sqn as 'GH' by 05.98 passing to both 5 Sqn and 56 [R] Sqn still in those marks. Returned to 43 Sqn by 02.02 and in 08.02 recoded 'XL'. Reverted to 'GH' by 08.04 before passing to 111 Sqn in 07.09. Flown to Leeming 09.09.09 for spares reclamation.
ZE839 AS082	First flew 10.11.88. Delivered to Leeming 25.11.88, and noted as 'EG'/23 Sqn 12.88. To 'FJ'/25 Sqn 09.90. Noted at Leuchars (still as 'FJ'/25 Sqn marks) 11.90, and operated by both 43 and 111 Sqns during its time there. Flown to Coningsby 05.08.91. becoming 'A6'/229 OCU the following month. To 'AR'/56 [R] Sqn (special marks consisting of a red fin and spine for 1993 display season) 04.93. to 111 Sqn by 11.98 taking up the code 'B'. To 5 Sqn as 'CH' by 09.00. First F.3 to undergo centre fuselage replacement, undertaking its air test on 31.08.01. To Coningsby 03.09.01 joining 5 Sqn by 05.92. Noted flying unmarked in 02.02. Recoded 'XK' in 10.02 before moving to Leeming, initially 11 Sqn, then 25 Sqn in 02.03. Next noted stored at St Athan in 03.06 and was at Leeming for RTP by 09.06.
ZE858 AS083	First Flew 17.11.88. Delivered to Leeming 15.12.88, and had the code 'FK' applied together with large question marks applied to the fin (due to the pending decision on the identity of the sixth Tornado F.3 squadron. The code 'FK' stands for something which is not printable!). To 'FB'/25 Sqn 07.89. To 43 Sqn (as 'FB'/25 Sqn marks) on 30.08.90. Operating with 111 Sqn during 04.91. Back with 43 Sqn during 07.91. Flown to Coningsby 31.08.91, to join 229 OCU as 'A5'. Operating with 43 Sqn during 05.92 (still coded 'A5'). To 'GO'/43 Sqn 06.93. W/o 21.10.93 when it crashed near Barnard Castle on the County Durham/Cumbria border following an in-flight fire.

A trio of jets in a perfect stacked echelon after in-flight refuelling. Flown by crews from No.111 Squadron on 20 July 2006, this shot shows just how difficult it was at times to keep track of individual aircraft allocations. ZE834/HD nearest the camera has the correct code applicable to the squadron markings. ZE810/XU is in No.43 (F) Squadron marks and still retaining the 2001 individual aircraft coding system, even though in March 2006 it had been allocated 'GG', and ZE289/VX is in 111 Squadron marks with an individual aircraft rather than squadron code.

ZE859 AS084	Diverted on the production line to Royal Saudi Air Force/29 Sqn as 2905 (build No.DS001). First flight 01.12.88, delivered 20.03.89.
ZE860 AS085	Diverted on the production line to Royal Saudi Air Porce/29 Sqn as 2906 (build No.DS002). First flight 22.12.88, delivered 20.03.89.
ZE861 AS086	Diverted on the production line to Royal Saudi Air Force/29 Sqn as 2901 (build No.DT001). First flight 30.01.89, delivered 20.03.89.
ZE862 AT034	First flight 02.12.88. Delivered to Coningsby 22.12.88, and was noted operating with the F3OEU 01.89. Passed to 56 [R] Sqn 01.12.95 but lost in a mid-air collision with ZE166/AF on 10.01.96, both aircraft crashing in the vicinity of Sleaford, Lincs.
ZE882 AS087	Diverted on the production line to Royal Saudi Air Force/29 Sqn as 2902 (build No.DT002). First flight 24.02.89, delivered 20.03.89.
ZE883 AS088	Diverted on the production line to Royal Saudi Air Force/29 Sqn as 2903 (build No.DT003). First flight 07.04.89, delivered 12.09.89.
ZE884 AS089	Diverted on the production line to Royal Saudi Air Force/29 Sqn as 2904 (build No.DT004). First flight 03.05.89, delivered 16.05.89.
ZE885 AS090	Diverted on the production line to Royal Saudi Air Force/29 Sqn as 2907 (build No.DS003). First flight 01.06.89, delivered 19.09.89.
ZE886 AS091	Diverted on the production line to Royal Saudi Air Force/29 Sqn as 2908 (build No.DS004). First flight 14.06.89, delivered 05.09.89.
ZE887 AS092	First flew 30.09.88. BAe trials a/c with A&AEE 12.88. Delivered to RAF 02.05.89 noted at Coningsby 06.89 (unmarked), becoming 'AN'/229 OCU during 07.89. To 'GE'/43 Sqn 01.90. To Leeming on I4.08.90, and became 'DE'/11 [C] Sqn by 10.09.90. Returned to 43 Sqn 24.09.90, and had lost its code by 29.10.90. Deployed to Dhahran as part of 43 [C] Sqn 11.01.91 (coded 'E' in theatre). Returned to Coningsby 13.03.91. Noted operating with 11 Sqn (still as 'E'/no marks) 04.91. To 'DJ'/11 Sqn 05.91. Deployed to Nellis AFB, NV for Exercise Red Flag 93/1 during 10.92. With 5 Sqn by 05.01 and recoded 'XJ'. Back to 11 Sqn by 06.03 and initially reverting back to its former 'DJ' code. Later adopted the stylised 'XI' code and received an all black tail. To 111 Sqn by 11.05 although back at Leeming in 06.06 and re-issued to 25 Sqn by 02.07. Noted coded 'FX' in 04.07 it soon received the squadron's '0th aniversary markings – 1915-2005' including the retention of the black tail. Later altered to read 1915-2008 to mark the Sqn's disbandment. To 43 Sqn by 05.08. Again the black tail was retained and the aircraft received special marks and the code 'GF'. To 111 Sqn at time of unit's disbandment retaining its former markings although allocated the code 'HG'. Stored at Leuchars for RAF, departing by road on 23.09.10.

ZE888 AT035	First flew 16.12.88 and delivered 30.01.89. First noted at Coningsby operating with the F3OEU during 02.89. Noted in the Leeming ASF 07.89, although had returned to the F3OEU during 08.89. Operated unmarked with 111 Sqn 06.90. To Leeming 23.08.90, becoming 'DT'/11 [C] Sqn two days later. Deployed to Dhahran 16.09.90. Recoded as 'I' with 43 [C] Sqn during 12.90. Returned to the UK (Leeming) 12.01.91, and operating with 11 Sqn by 19.01.91 (still as 'I'/no marks). Noted in the Leuchars ASF during 02.91, although back at Leeming later that month for service with 23 Sqn. To 'EV'/23 Sqn 05.91. Loaned to 111 Sqn 01.92, passing to 43 Sqn 04.92. Returned to 23 Sqn 05.92. To 'FV'/25 Sqn by 09.94, it was transferred to 111 Sqn in 10.97 although retained its former markings. Recoded 'HT' in 06.98 and later just 'T' it remained with the unit until passing to 56 [R] Sqn in 02.02 as 'AN'. Later recoded 'TC' it was wfu at Leuchars in 11.07 and taken by road to Shawbury for storage on 09.05.08. Later to Leeming for RTP on 16.04.09.
ZE889 AS093	First flight 21.02.89 and delivered to Coningsby 03.04.89 flying with the F3OEU 08.89. Received the 'AWC' markings in 08.94 and coded 'SB' for Stuart Black, the squadron commander. To Leeming 08.96 and then to 1435 Flt on 23.09.98 as 'H' ('Hope'). Returned 17.04.00 to Coningsby but then passed to 111 Sqn by 02.01. With 56 [R] Sqn as 'XI' in 09.02 until wfu at Leuchars in 01.06 for spares recovery.
ZE890 AS094	Diverted on the production line to Royal Saudi Air Force/29 Sqn as 2909 (build No.DS005). First flight 27.07.89, delivered 05.09.89.
ZE891 AS095	Diverted on the production line to Royal Saudi Air Force/29 Sqn as 2910 (build No.DS006). First flight 08.08.89, delivered 12.09.89.
ZE905 AS096	Diverted on the production line to Royal Saudi Air Force/29 Sqn as 2911 (build No.DS007). First flight 15.08.89, delivered 05.09.89.
ZE906 AS097	Diverted on the production line to Royal Saudi Air Force/29 Sqn as 2912 (build No.DS008). First flight 24.08.89, delivered 19.09.89. Written off in a crash 08.11.98.

Clearly straight off the wash rack, ZE907 in the new darker grey colour scheme and black markings is seen landing at RAF Waddington on 13 September 2006. It will be noted that the aircraft has No.25 Squadron marks on the fin yet carries a No.XI Squadron code. At the time it was on the strength of No.25 Squadron and had been assigned the code 'FN' but it is not clear whether this was ever applied before its transfer to 111 Squadron the following year.

ZE907 AS098	First flew 02.02.89. Delivered to Coningsby 03.04.89, and had become 'CH'/5 Sqn by the end of that month; with 229 OCU by 02.90 wearing special marks for the 1990 display season (consisting of red/white chevrons on fin and spine, with red cheatlines on the undersides and Battle of Britain 50th Anniversary motif on nose). To Leeming 21.08.90, becoming 'DK'/11 [C] Sqn by 02.09.90. Deployed to Dhahran 22.09.90. Recoded as 'K' whilst still in theatre with 43 [C] Sqn by 01.91. Returned to the UK during late 02.91. To 'EN'/23 Sqn by 06.91. Took part in Exercise Red Flag 93/1 at Nellis AFB, NV during 10–11.92. To 'FM'/25 Sqn by 10.94 then 'GL'/43 Sqn in 05.98. Returned to Leeming for 11 Sqn and recoded 'XH' by 01.04. Recoded again in 11.03 to 'XI' in 06.04 when on loan to FJWOEU. Still with 11 Sqn it was recoded again to 'DA' in 04.05; it later passed to 25 Sqn where it was assigned 'FN' but not reported as ever carried. To 111 Sqn 06.07 and allocated the code 'HK' but passed into store at Leuchars in 12.08 and taken by road to Leeming for RTP on 17.04.09.
ZE908 AT036	First flew 03.04.89 and delivered 24.09.89 although had been sighted at Coningsby as 'CJ'/5 Sqn 06.89, but operated with 229 OCU until 11.89. Recoded as 'CT' with 5 Sqn during 12.89. To Leeming by 16.08.90 to become 'DU'/11 [C] Sqn by 25.08.90. Uncoded by 13.09.90, and transferred to 43 Sqn on 24.09.90. Deployed to Dhahran 18.11.90, and became 'X'/43 [C] Sqn in theatre. Returned to the UK mid-03.91, and noted flying with 25 Sqn during late 03.91 (still coded 'X'). To 'FC'/25 Sqn 06.91. Loaned to 5 Sqn 06.09.93–11.93. To 111 Sqn as 'HV' when deployed to Butterworth for Exercise Flying Fish in 04.97. Recoded 'TB' it was with 11 Sqn in 06.02 and 56 [R] Sqn in 09.02. It was placed in store at St Athan by 08.05 and reduced to spares and eventually scrapped.
ZE909 AS099	Diverted on the production line to Royal Saudi Air Force/34 Sqn as 3451 (build No.DT005). First flight 03.09.89, delivered 14.11.89. Later transferred to 29 Sqn as 2913.
ZE910 AS100	Diverted on the production line to Royal Saudi Air Force/34 Sqn as 3452 (build No.DT006). First flight 07.12.89, delivered 13.03.89. Later transferred to 29 Sqn as 2914.
ZE911 AS101	First flew 12.04.89. Delivered to Coningsby 27.04.89, and with the F3OEU by 07.89. Passed to 29 Sqn (unmarked) 11.91, becoming 'BE' in 12.91. Loaned to the Leeming Wing during 11.93. To 43 Sqn by 05.95 and coded 'GA' in 08.95. To AMI loan programme as MM7226/5321, it was rolled out at St Athan on 23.12.96. Later recoded 3621 to return to St Athan at the end of the lease period on 07.06.04 where it was recovered for spares in 08.04. Hulk dispatched for scrap by road on 23.09.04.
ZE912 AS102	Diverted on the production line to Royal Saudi Air Force/34 Sqn as 3453 (build No.DS009). First flight 13.12.89, delivered 13.03.89 but later transferred to 29 Sqn as 2915.
ZE913 AS103	Diverted on the production line to Royal Saudi Air Force/34 Sqn as 3454 (build No.DS010). First flight 13.10.89, delivered 14.11.89. Later transferred to 29 Sqn as 2916.
ZE914 AS104	Diverted on the production line to Royal Saudi Air Force/34 Sqn as 3455 (build No.DS011). First flight 13.11.89, delivered 18.12.89. Later transferred to 29 Sqn as 2917 but wfu and is now preserved.
ZE934 ATO37	First flew 15.05.89 and delivered 25.05.89. First sighted at Coningsby as 'CE'/5 Sqn 06.89. Transferred to 111 Sqn 06.90 (still as 'CE'). To Leeming by 15.08.90, and became 'DV'/11[C] Sqn by 27.08.90; acted as airspare for the Granby" deployment on 29.08.90; passed to 43 Sqn (still coded 'DV') by 25.09.90. Noted operating from Coningsby (uncoded) late 11.90. Deployed to Dhahran 11.01.91, and became 'Q' with 43[C] Sqn in theatre; returned to the UK (Leeming) by 23.02.91, and operating with 23 Sqn by the end of that month (still coded 'Q'). To 'DX'/11 Sqn 04.91. Remained with squadron until transfer to 111 Sqn as 'HS' in 10.97 later recoded 'S'. It had deployed with 111 Sqn to Butterworth unmarked in 04.97. To 'AP/56[R]' Sqn by 11.00 but later recoded 'TA' in 05.02. To 11 Sqn by 03.04 but then wfu and sent to East Fortune for preservation and display on 13.09.05.
ZE935 AS105	Diverted on the production line to Royal Saudi Air Porce/34 Sqn as 3456 (build No.DS012). First flight 15.12.89 delivered 04.06.90. Later transferred to 29 Sqn as 2918.
ZE936 AS106	First flew 25.04.89. Delivered 11.05.89. First noted unmarked at Coningsby 06.89, and flying with the F3OEU 08.89. To 25 Sqn (still unmarked) 09.89. To 'GK'/43 Sqn 04.90. To Leeming on 11.08.90, and took up the code 'DF' with 11[C] Sqn by 25.08.90. Deployed to Dhahran 29.08.90; . became 'F' with 43[C] Sqn 12.90 (in theatre); returned to the UK (Leeming) 12.01.91, and flying as 'F' with 11 Sqn a week later. To 'EE'/23 Sqn 04.91; loaned to 111 Sqn 03.92, and deployed to Eielson AFB, AK as part of Exercise Distant Frontier 92 on 06.04.92; returned to 23 Sqn 05.92. Deployed to Malaysia under Exercise IADS 92 during 09.92. Deployed to Gioia del Colle AB, Italy under Operation "Grapple" 19.04.93 (returned during 05.93). To 'DL/11' Sqn where it received the 'Black Sheep Brewery' badge on the port side of the fin plus a line drawing of a leaping ram to mark the squadrons connection with the Theakston Brewery in Masham. To 'XF/5' Sqn in 07.01 then to 25 Sqn by 10.02 before returning to 11 Sqn. Re-assigned to 111 Sqn by 04.03 but initially operated in 11 Sqn marks it was coded 'HE' in 11.04. After a period acting as the Leuchars WLT airframe in 03.06 it was RTS in 05.06. Finally wfu in 10.09 whilst still with 111 Sqn and sent to Leeming for RTP.
ZE937 AS107	Diverted on the production line to Royal Saudi Air Force/34 Sqn as 3457 (build No.DS013), First flight 05.02.90 delivered 30.04.90. Transferred to 29 Sqn as 2919.
ZE938 AS108	Diverted on the production line to Royal Saudi Air Force/34 Sqn as 3458 (build No.DS014), First flight 09.03.90 delivered 30.04.90. Transferred to 29 Sqn as 2920.
ZE939 AS109	Diverted on the production line to Royal Saudi Air Force/34 Sqn as 3459 (build No.DS015), First flight 14.05.90 delivered 20.08.90. Transferred to 29 Sqn as 2921.
ZE940 AS110	Diverted on the production line to Royal Saudi Air Force/34 Sqn as 3460 (build No.DS016), First flight 22.06.90 delivered 27.08.90. Transferred to 29 Sqn as 2922.

ZE941 AT038	First flew 22.05.89 and delivered 21.06.89. First noted at Coningsby (unmarked) during 07.89, and noted in use with the F3OEU by 10.89. By 01.90 to 5 Sqn (unmarked), eventually becoming 'CI' with the unit by 04.90. To Leeming by 15.08.90, and became 'DW'/11 [C] Sqn by 26.08.90. Deployed to Dhahran 22.09.90. Returned to the UK (Leuchars) on 19.11.90 (still coded 'DW'). Noted unmarked in the Leuchars ASF 01.91. To 11 Sqn as 'R'/no marks by 19.02.91. Returned to Coningsby 13.03.91 with the 29 Sqn element of 43 [C] Sqn (believed not to have deployed to the Gulf but only to Decimomannu). Back with 11 Sqn (again as 'R') late 03.91. To 'DY'/11 Sqn 05.91. To 'FE'/25 Sqn 04.93. To 43 Sqn 09.97 and assigned code 'GI' but thought to have never been carried. Back with 25 Sqn as 'FE' in 10.98 and to 56 [R] Sqn by 05.02, later taking up the code 'KT' by 06.02. To 43 Sqn in 05.05 but placed into short-term store at Leuchars in 06.06. Re-issued to 111 Sqn 12.06 but stored again in 12.08. To Leeming by road 21.04.09 for RTP.
ZE942 AS111	First flew 19.05.89. Delivered 25.07.89. First noted 06.89 at the Paris Salon at Le Bourget as part of the BAe static display. Next seen unmarked at Coningsby during 07.89, and in use with 5 Sqn the following month (still devoid of marks). Passed to 43 Sqn 01.90, and became 'GH' with the unit by 03.90. To Leeming on 11.08.90, and took up the code 'DG' with 11 [C] Sqn by 26.08.90. Flown to Dhahran 16.09.90. Returned to the UK (Leuchars) via Paris-Orly (technical diversion) 21.11.90, and in use with 111 Sqn (as 'DO') during 01.91. Transferred to 11 Sqn as 'F'/no marks by 19.02.91. To 'DK'/11 Sqn 05.91. Loaned to 5 Sqn 06.09.93–11.93. With AWC in 03.98 but back with 5 Sqn as 'CM' in 06.00. Noted flying unmarked in 02.02, it was recoded 'XE' in 05.02 and passed to 11 Sqn where it took up the code 'DF' in 06.05. Later to 111 Sqn by 11.05 with whom it suffered a bird strike in 05.07 following which it was wfu and dispatched to Leeming in 08.07 for RTP.
ZE943 AS112	Diverted on the production line to Royal Saudi Air Force/34 Sqn as 3461 (build No.DS017). First flight 20.07.90, delivered 27.08.90. Later transferred to 29 Sqn as 2923.
ZE960 AS113	Diverted on the production line to Royal Saudi Air Force/34 Sqn as 3462 (build No.DS018), First flight 24.09.90, delivered 08.10.90. Later transferred to 29 Sqn as 2924.
ZE961 AS114	First flew 11.07.89 and delivered 28.07.89. First seen at Coningsby during early 08.89 (unmarked), becoming 'GA'/43 Sqn by 14.09.89 (the first aircraft for that squadron). Delivered to Leuchars 23.09.89. To Leeming on 11.08.90, becoming 'DH'/11 [C] Sqn by 26.08.90. Deployed to Dhahran 29.08.90. Recoded by 43 [C] Sqn as 'H' in theatre; returned to the UK (Coningsby) 13.03.91. To 25 Sqn, as 'H'/no marks, late 03.91. To 'FD'/25 Sqn 07.91. Loaned to 111 Sqn 03.92 and deployed to Alaska as part of Exercise Distant Frontier 92 on 06.04.92. Returned to 25 Sqn 05.92. Deployed to Nellis AFB, NV for Exercise Red Flag 93/1 during 10–11.92. Deployed to Italy for Operation Grapple 19.04.93. To 25 Sqn as 'FT' by 02.96. Later to 56 [R] Sqn and coded 'AW' in 02.01 but recoded 'XD' in 03.02. To 25 Sqn by 10.03, eventually taking up the code 'FO'. Transferred to 43 Sqn by 03.08 and allocated the code 'GR' but not clear if ever carried. Passed to 111 Sqn where it was allocated the code 'HB' but again unclear whether carried. Placed in short-term store at Leuchars in 07.09 but RTS in 09.09 as 'HB' and is still current.

January 2006, on refuelling area 5, Tristar KC.1 ZD950 refuels a Tornado F.3 from 111 Squadron, ZE962/XC, while another example, ZE288/VX, awaits its turn. On the starboard wing is Tornado GR.4A ZA401 in the XIII Squadron 90th anniversary colour scheme.

ZE962 AS115	First flew 18.07.89 and delivered 28.07.89. First noted at Coningsby during 08.89, becoming 'GB'/43 Sqn later that month prior to delivery to Leuchars on 23.09.89. Flown to Leeming on 14.08.90, and took up the code 'DI' with 11 [C] Sqn by 25.08.90. Deployed to Dhahran 29.08.90; recoded as 'I'/43 [C] Sqn during 12.90 whilst still in theatre. Returned to Leeming 12.01.91, and in use with 11 Sqn (as 'I') by 16.01.91. To 'FJ'/25 Sqn 06.91. Deployed to Nellis AFB, NV as part of Exercise Red Flag 93/1 during 10–11.92. Became the first aircraft to receive the revised No.25 Sqn markings of a black silhouette of the current insignia falcon sitting atop a gauntlet along with white code letters. Operated unmarked throughout 1998. To 5 Sqn by 01.02. Recoded 'XC' and then loaned to 111 Sqn where it received fin marking only. Took part in second Gulf campaign deployment, receiving nose art as described elsewhere in 04.03. Lost on 14.10.05 in a crash 10 miles south east of Leuchars following loss of control. The subsequent investigation to determine the cause saw the airframe recovered although due to the severity of the impact this comprised of around only 50 per cent.
ZE963 AT039	First flew 11.08.89. Delivered to Leuchars 23.08.89 for engineering familiarisation, and noted operating unmarked with 43 Sqn during the following month. To 'GC'/43 Sqn 01.90. To Leeming by 26.08.90 when noted as 'DX'/11 [C] Sqn. Acted as airspare for the Granby deployment on 16.09.90, itself deploying on 22.09.90. Returned to the UK (Leuchars) 20.11.90 still coded as 'DX' (still present in the ASF there between 01–02.91). To 23 Sqn (unmarked) 03.91, and became 'ET' with the unit during 04.91. Loaned to 43 Sqn during 03.92, returning to 23 Sqn 05.92. Loaned to 29 Sqn during 10.92. Transferred to 'GE'/43 Sqn by 10.97 and recoded 'YT' by 08.02. To 56 [R] Sqn by 03.04 and placed in store at Leeming 27.06.06. Re-issued to 43 Sqn in 2009 but flown to Leeming for RTP 17.08.09.

ZE964 AT040	First flew 27.09.89. Delivered to Leuchars 17.10.89. Operating with 43 Sqn (unmarked) by 12.89. Flown to Leeming on 22.08.90 to become 'DS' with 11 [C] Sqn (noted as such 31.08.90). Acted as Granby deployment airspare on 22.09.90, and had transferred to 43 Sqn by 25.09.90 (still coded 'DS'). To Coningsby (uncoded) by 08.11.90, and joined the F3OEU later that month. To 'X'/no marks with 11 Sqn by 05.02.91, switching to 'J'/no marks with 23 Sqn during 03.91. To 'EU'/23 Sqn 04.91. To 'DY'/11 Sqn 03.93. Took part in the static display for the Royal Review at Marham on 01.04.93. Deployed to Gioia del Colle, Italy for Operation Grapple on 19.04.93. To 43 Sqn initially as 'GM' then later 'GN'. With 25 Sqn in 01.01, 5 Sqn in 08.01 but loaned to 56 [R] Sqn in 02.02 before returning to 5 Sqn by 05.02. By road to St Athan 20.06.02 before RTS with 56 [R] Sqn. Coded 'XT' with 111 Sqn and later 11 Sqn in 10.04. Entered RTP at Leeming 08.12.08.
ZE965 AT041 (Originally AS117)	First flew 23.10.89 and delivered 02.11.89. First noted operating unmarked with 43 Sqn during 01.90, transferred to 111 Sqn by 06.90. To 'HA'/111 Sqn early 08.90, although flown to Leeming on 15.08.90 to join 11 [C] Sqn as 'DY' (noted as such 25.08.90). Acted as airspare for the Granby deployment on 22.09.90, and returned to 43 Sqn (still coded 'DY') by 25.09.90. Noted uncoded at Leuchars by 29.10.90. To Coningsby by 20.11.90 (being operated unmarked by 29 Sqn). To 11 Sqn as 'Y'/no marks by 06.01.91, being recoded as 'V' by 05.02.91. Back to 29 Sqn (still coded 'V') by 06.91. Becoming 'BZ' with the unit by 08.91. To 'DW'/11 Sqn 05.93. Loaned to 5 Sqn 06.09.93-11.93. O/L to DERA 09.94 and issued to 43 Sqn as 'GM' in 09.97. To 56 [R] Sqn 10.01 before coding 'WT'. Finally to 111 Sqn 01.09 receiving code 'HZ' but flown to Leeming for RTP 13.10.10.
ZE966 AT042 (Originally AS118)	First flew 27.11.89. Delivered to Leuchars 09.01.90 (800th production Tornado and 160th ADV model). To 'GF'/43 Sqn late 01.90, with special black/white checks on fin for the squadron CO (the code 'GF' just happens to coincide with the unit's 'Gloria Finis' motto). Flown to Leeming on 22.08.90, and seen as 'DZ'/11 [C] Sqn on 30.08.90; returned to 43 Sqn by 01.10.90, when seen uncoded. To Coningsby 08.11.90. Noted operating unmarked with 111 Sqn during early 01.91. Transferred to 11 Sqn coded 'Y' by 22.01.91. Noted in the Leuchars ASF early 02.91, and deployed to Dhahran later that month apparently wearing 'GF'/43 Sqn marks at the request of OC 43 [C] Sqn. Returned to Leuchars 13.03.91. Operating with 11 Sqn (as 'GF'/43 Sqn marks) 04.91, becoming 'DZ' with the unit during 05.91. Loaned to 29 Sqn during 10.92. Recoded 'DXI' in 03.98 but reverted to 'DX' by 06.99. Recoded 'VT' then used by 25 Sqn, 56 [R] Sqn in 10.02 and 111 Sqn in 06.04. Fuselage noted stored at St Athan 01.07 and later given to the Museum of Science and Industry in Manchester during 11.07, although is currently stored at Swinton.
ZE967 AT043 (Originally AS119)	First flight 07.12.89 and delivered 20.12.89. First noted at Leuchars during 01.90 (unmarked), and joined 43 Sqn that month. To Leeming by 02.09.90 when noted as 'DR'/11 [C] Sqn. Returned to 43 Sqn by 25.09.90, and lost its code by 29.10.90. To Coningsby 20.11.90 for use by the F3OEU. To 'U'/no marks with 11 Sqn by 13.02.91. Operating with 25 Sqn (still as 'U') during 04.91, becoming 'FE' with the squadron later that month. To 'EU'/23 Sqn by 02.93. To 25 Sqn as 'FU' by 05.94, then 111 Sqn as 'UT' although operated unmarked with Leuchars wing in 09.00 before issue to 43 Sqn in 02.02. Transferred to 56 [R] Sqn by 03.03 until retired and placed on display at RAF Leuchars in 03.05.
ZE968 AS120	First flight 22.02.90. Delivered to Leuchars 13.03.90 but returned to Warton. Re-delivered 14.05.90. Painted as 'HE'/111 Sqn at Coningsby by mid-06.90, returned to Leuchars on 20.06.90. Flown to Leeming on 20.08.90, becoming 'DJ'/11 [C] Sqn by 25.08.90. Deployed to Dhahran 29.08.90, and wore the 'Desert Eagles - Royal Air Force' insignia atop the fin. Recoded as 'J' in theatre by 43 [C] Sqn during 12.90. Returned to the UK (possibly to Coningsby on 13.03.91). Recoded as 'I'/no marks and operating with 29 Sqn during late 03.91. Operating with 229 OCU by 08.91 (still as 'I'). To 'BA'/29 Sqn 09.91, although transferred to the F3OEU by 12.91 (eventually lost its former unit's marks/code during 01.92). Received 'AWC' marks in 09.94 but transferred to 11 Sqn as 'DM' by 06.96. To 43 Sqn as 'GV' then in 03.98 'GN'. Back with 11 Sqn 07.99 operating uncoded but allocated 'DM', but not clear whether carried. Recoded 'XB' and with 111 Sqn in 10.02. Deployed as part of second Gulf campaign, receiving nose art as described elsewhere. Retained by 111 Sqn and coded 'HB' in 06.04 but noted unmarked in 01.08. Placed in store at Leuchars in 05.09 and flown to Leeming for RTP 03.06.09.
ZE969 AS121	First flight 03.05.90. Delivered to Leuchars 06.06.90, becoming 'HD' with 111 Sqn later that month. Flown to Leeming on 19.08.90, joining 11 [C] Sqn as 'DL' by 30.08.90. Deployed to Dhahran 16.09.90. Recoded as 'L' by 43 [C] Sqn during 12.90. Returned to the UK (Coningsby) on 14.03.91. To 23 Sqn (still as 'L'/no marks) during 04.91, although operated for a time by 11 Sqn during the month. To 'EA'/23 Sqn 05.91. Flew to Malaysia for Exercise IADS 92 during 09.92. Loaned to 29 Sqn during 11.93. Re-assigned to 11 Sqn as 'DI' 06.94 and then later 'DJ'. Un-coded in 02.99 and flown to Falkland Islands for 1435 Flt 04.00 becoming 'F' ('Faith'). Returned to UK 30.05.01 and re-assigned to 56 [R] Sqn becoming 'XA' in 07.01. To 25 Sqn by 10.02 and coded 'FH' in 02.06. Back with 56 [R] Sqn in 01.08 before transfer to 111 Sqn where it was allocated the code 'HQ'. Placed in store at Leuchars 05.09 and flown to Leeming for RTP 10.06.09.
ZE982 AS122	First flight 01.06.90 Delivered to Leeming 28.08.90 direct from Warton with Stage 1+ modofications. To 'DP'/11 [C] Sqn by 07.09.90, and flew to Dhahran 16.09.90. Recoded as 'P' in theatre with 43 [C] Sqn during 12.90. Returned to the UK (Leeming) 12.02.91, and flying with 11 Sqn (still as 'P'/no marks) by 25.02.91. Operated with 25 Sqn during 04.91, returning again to 11 Sqn as 'DM' during 05.91. Deployed to Nellis AFB, NV during 10–11.92 for Exercise Red Flag 93/1. Loaned to 5 Sqn 07.09.93–11.93. To F3OEU by 12.95 and sent to 1435 Flt by An-124 17.01.00 only to return by same method 17.04.00. To 'CP'/5 Sqn 09.00 with new style markings. Recoded 'VV' in 08.01 before passing to 25 Sqn by 06.02. Recoded 'FR' by 03.06 and to 43 Sqn by 04.08. Lost in a crash on 02.07.09 in Glen Kinglas, Argyleshire, having flown 4201.45 hours total.
ZE983 AS123	First flew 24.10.90. Delivered 13.11.90 to Leuchars. noted as 'B'/no marks with 11 Sqn during 01.91 (having been re-delivered from Warton earlier that month), uncoded with the squadron by 05.02.91. To 'EZ'/23 Sqn 04.91. Flown to Malaysia for Exercise IADS 92 during 09.92. With 111 Sqn as 'HP' in 08.94, then 'DN'/11 Sqn in 11.96 and is believed to have swapped tail fins with ZE736/HA in 07.98. Recoded 'WY' in 02.02 and passed to 43 Sqn in 10.02. Returned to 111 Sqn by 01.03 still as 'WY' which it retained until at least 03.08 and then allocated code 'HL'. Noted so coded by 11.09 and current with the unit.

ZG728 AS124	First flight 10.12.90. First seen 09.90 as part of the BAe contingent at the Farnborough SBAC Airshow. Delivered to Coningsby 10.12.90, and noted as 'CI' with 5 Sqn late 01.91. Loaned to 11 Sqn during 10.92, returning to 5 Sqn 11.92. Loaned to Leeming Wing 11.93. Selected as part of AMI loan programme becoming MM7229/5306 but later recoded to 3607. Returned to St Athan at end of lease period on 04.12.03 for spares recovery in 12.04. Fuselage noted stored 08.05 and again in 01.07. Eventually disposed of for scrap to M. Williams & Sons, Hitchin, on 04.10.07.
ZG730 AS125	First flight 16.11.90 and delivered to Coningsby 10.01.90. First noted as 'CC'/5 Sqn during 03.91. Selected for AMI loan programme and flown to St Athan 12.03.96. Became MM7230/5307 but later recoded 3611. Returned to St Athan at end of lease period on 28.07.04 for spares recovery in 11.04. Hulk (forward fuselage only) disposed of for scrap 11.01.05 to Beaver Metals, Water Orton where noted in 02.05. Report of centre fuselage being stored at St Athan in 04.05.
ZG731 AS126	First flight 24.11.90. Delivered to Coningsby 14.12.90, becoming 'CG' with 5 Sqn by 02.91. Deployed to Alaska for Exercise Distant Frontier 93 during 04.93. Loaned to the Leeming Wing 11.93. To 'BL/29' Sqn by 06.96 then with 56 [R] Sqn 10.98. Assigned to 111 Sqn and allocated the code 'H' in 10.98, it seems that it retained the 29 Sqn marks being so noted later. Loaned to BAE Systems in 06.99 and alternated between them and the F3OEU with whom it adopted marks comprising of a winged sword in a red disc. Coded 'WV' in 02.02 still with the FJWOEU and then subsequently 41 Sqn. To 111 Sqn 08.04.08 before entering Leuchars store in 12.08. To Leeming for RTP 24.06.09.
ZG732 AS127	First flight 30.05.91. First recorded as 'BC'/29 Sqn during 07.91. Loaned to the Leeming Wing 11.93 before being selected as part of the AMI loan programme. Became MM7227/5305 before recoding to 3622. Returned to UK at St Athan at end of lease period on 04.08.03 before re-allocated to 56 [R] Sqn as 'WU' in 12.03. Noted stored at St Athan 03.06 and again in 01.07.
ZG733 AS128	Delivered 23.05.91. First seen with 29 Sqn as 'BK' during 06.91. Flown to Eielson AFB, Alaska for Exercise Distant Frontier 93 during 04.93. Loaned to the Leeming Wing in 11.93. To 56 [R] Sqn 08.96 and allocated 'AO'. Became 'AC' in 10.96 before being selected for AMI loan programme. To MM7228/5303 before recoding to 3634. Returned to UK at St Athan at end of lease period on 23.10.03 for spares recovery. Disposed of for scrap on 03.11.04.
ZG734 AS129	Delivered 07.06.91. First noted operating unmarked with 29 Sqn during 07.91. To 'BG'/29 Sqn during 01.92. Loaned to 11 Sqn during 11.92. Deployed for Exercise Distant Frontier 93 to Alaska during 04.93. Recoded as 'BA' with 29 Sqn during 07.93. Selected as part of the AMI loan programme becoming MM7231/5311. Returned to St Athan at end of lease period in 2003 for spares recovery. Noted stored in 04.05 and 01.07. Eventually disposed of for scrap to M. Williams & Sons, Hitchin, on 04.10.07.
ZG735 AS130	Delivered to Coningsby 05.07.91 becoming 'CO'/5 Sqn during 08.91. Loaned to 11 Sqn during 10.92, returning 11.92. Loaned to the Leeming Wing 11.93. Assigned to 1435 Flt 03.04.95 but returned to UK for re-issue to 56 Sqn as 'AZ' in 06.96. Loaned to AWC in 07.96 before being selected for AMI loan programme where it become MM7232/5310 before recoding to 3610. Returned to UK at St Athan at end of lease period for spares recovery. Noted dumped in 03.05 and fuselage eventually disposed of for scrapping on 27.10.05.
ZG751 AS131	First flight 11.07.91. Delivered to Coningsby 14.08.91. To 'CW'/5 Sqn by 10.91, and loaned to 11 Sqn as such during 10.92; reportedly sustained CAT 3 damage and at the Coningsby ASF since 06.93. RTS with 56 [R] Sqn by 02.95 coded 'AW'. Sent to Falkland Islands for 1435 Flt 21.09.96 as 'C' ('Charity') returning to the UK by 03.98. Again with 56 [R] Sqn as 'AV' in 10.98 but still sporting 1435 Flt markings. To 5 Sqn 03.99 and allocated code 'CJ' but loaned to 25 Sqn in 04.99. 'CO'/5 Sqn in 08.99 before transfer to 111 Sqn in those marks. Recoded 'WP' in 10.01 and with 11 Sqn in 05.03. Aircraft aquaplaned on landing at CFB Goose Bay 25.08.03 during Exercise Western Strike, causing the crew to eject. Returned to the UK by C-17A 29.09.03, arriving at St Athan by road 03.10.03. RTS with 43 Sqn by 03.05 but returned to 1435 Flt by An-124 (RA-82014) on 16.04.05 becoming 'D' ('Desperation'). Returned to UK 06.07 and allocated to 111 Sqn still in 1435 Flt markings, although assigned the code 'HI'. To 43 Sqn by 11.08 until placed in store at Leuchars in 12.08 before being flown to Leeming for RTP 20.01.09.
ZG753 AS132	First flight 23.09.91. Delivered to Coningsby 08.10.91, and flying unmarked with 5 Sqn later that month. To 'CH'/5 Sqn during 11.91. To 1435 Flt 01.94 as 'C' ('Charity'), returning to UK 14.04.95. Assigned to 56 [R] Sqn as 'AF' but returned to 1435 Flt by 01.96, this time as 'F' ('Faith'). Returned to UK by 05.97 following an emergency diversion into Ascension Island on 15.05.97 during the swap over. Air-freighted to Cardiff then by road to St Athan on 21.07.95. Reports indicated major component damage and suggested rear fuselage utilised to repair ZE163 with remainder in store between 08.99 and 09.00. However noted on air test 01.08.01 and flown to Leeming 13.08.01 coded 'WO'. Returned to 1435 Flt by C-17A 27.11.01, later returning to UK for 111 Sqn as 'HH' being so noted in Leuchars ASF. Once again to 1435 Flt on 10.01.08 becoming 'H' ('Hope') becoming the last Tornado F.3 to serve in the Falklands. Returned to Leeming for RTP in 10.09.
ZG755 AS133	First flew 11.10.91. Delivered to Leuchars 11.11.91, becoming 'GM'/43 Sqn that month. Took part in Kuwait Liberation 1st Anniversary Flypast 22–27.02.92. Unmarked with 43 Sqn by 02.93, transferring to 5 Sqn later that month. To 29 Sqn 03.93, still unmarked, but allocated the code 'BB'. Took part in Exercise Distant Frontier 93 in Alaska during 04.93. To 1435 Flt 06.94 until 27.10.95 returning to 56 [R] Sqn allocated the code 'AY'. 29 Sqn as 'BJ' by 03.96. 'CD'/5 Sqn by 10.98 followed a period of use by 111 Sqn unmarked before transfer to 56 [R] Sqn 01.01. To 25 Sqn by 05.01 and 11 Sqn 02.02. Initially uncoded but with revised unit insignia eventually coded 'WN' until 10.04 when recoded 'DL'. To 43 Sqn 11.05 becoming 'GL' by 02.06. To 1435 Flt again 25.09.08 as 'F' ('Faith') returning to UK on final Tornado F.3 deployment to the Falkland Islands in 10.09. To Leeming for RTP by 11.09.

ZG757 AS134	First flew 20.11.91. Delivered to Leuchars 16.12.91, becoming 'HL'/111 Sqn during 01.92. To 'CA'/5 Sqn by late 02.93 (no marks). Loaned to the Leeming Wing 11.93. Still being operated as 'CA'/5 Sqn in 01.98. With 43 Sqn in 01.99 before transfer to 111 Sqn as 'U'. A period of loan to 25 Sqn followed and then 11 Sqn in 09.01 where it was coded 'WM'. Transferred to 43 Sqn 11.02 becoming 'GN' by 11.04. Received squadron's 90th anniversary markings in 07.06 complete with black tail. Wfu at Leuchars in 04.08 and flown to Leeming for RTP by 15.05.08.
ZG768 AS135	First flew 21.11.91. Delivered to Coningsby 11.12.91, flying unmarked with 229 OCU by 01.92. To 'AX'/56 [R] Sqn by 11.92 (no marks). Identified as part of the AMI loan programme becoming MM7233/5304. Returned to UK at end of lease period and underwent spares recovery at St Athan in 03.05. Fuselage noted dumped 08.05 and again in 01.07 before being disposed of for scrap on 04.10.07 to M. Williams & Sons, Hitchin.
ZG770 AS136	First flight 28.11.91. Delivered to Coningsby 11.12.91. Flying unmarked with 229 OCU during 01.92. To 'AP'/56 [R] Sqn 07.92 (first aircraft to carry the unit's marks following transition from 229 OCU/65 Sqn). To 'BD'/29' Sqn by 07.94 then to 5 Sqn as 'CC' by 10.99. Took part in a ground race with a Ducati motorcycle at Coningsby on 01.10.99. To 56 [R] Sqn as 'WK' by 05.02 before passing to 25 Sqn. Reported as wfu by 09.05 and stored at Leeming awaiting RTP.
ZG772 AS137	First flew 06.12.91. Delivered to Coningsby 20.12.91, noted unmarked during 01.92. To 'CN'/5 Sqn 03.92. to 1435 Flt 01.94 until 14.04.95 returning to UK and issue to 56 [R] Sqn. Again to 1435 Flt 25.09.99 and upon return to UK assigned code 'WJ'. Issued to 11 Sqn by 05.02 before once again heading to 1435 Flt on 09.09.02 by C-17A becoming 'C' ('Charity'). Upon return to UK in 03.05, taken by road to Leuchars and assigned 'GS'/43 Sqn. To 56 [R] Sqn 06.05 before being placed in store at Leuchars in 11.08. To Leeming by road 19.08.09 for RTP.
ZG774 AS138	First flew 26.02.92. Delivered 25.03.92 and noted unmarked with 43 Sqn during 03.92, becoming 'GW' by 04.92. Again unmarked in 03.93. To 'A4'/56 [R] Sqn 07.93. Later to 'AY' with 56 [R] Sqn and then 'BE'/29 Sqn in 01.95. Loaned to 111 Sqn before transfer to 'CG'/5 Sqn in 09.97. To 1435 Flt 09.99 where it suffered CAT 3 damage and was returned to the UK by An-124 on 27.01.00. Placed in store at St Athan where noted in 09.00 but RTS by 10.02 when it was with 11 Sqn as 'WI'. To 56 [R] Sqn as the 2005 display mount coded 'WK'. To 'GV'/43 Sqn by 05.08 until transfer to 111 Sqn in 07.09 where it became 'HM' and is still current.
ZG776 AS139	First flight 03.04.92. Delivered to Leuchars 30.04.92, becoming 'HN'/111 Sqn special marks by 06.92 (black fin/spine, gold panel on fin in which was the unit's standard insignia and code 'HN' in black). Unmarked with 111 Sqn during 02.93. To 29 Sqn 04.93 (still unmarked). Deployed to Alaska for Exercise Distant Frontier 93 during 04.93. Took up the code 'BD' with 29 Sqn 07.93. To 1435 Flt 06.94 as 'H' ('Hope') returning to UK 27.10.95 and issued to 56 [R] Sqn as 'AB' by 02.97. Again to 1435 Flt on 24.09.98 returning by An-124 27.01.00. Stored St Athan 09.00 before issue to 56 [R] Sqn. To 1435 Flt 23.05.01 where it received new style unit markings comprising of red and white fin band with Maltese Cross superimposed in the centre, returning to UK by 06.03. Allocated code 'WH' and with 111 Sqn in 10.03 still 1435 Flt markings. Once more to 1435 Flt this time by C-17A on 18.03.05. Returned to UK in 06.07 and taken by road to Leeming for RTP.

The 138th 'AS' version of the Tornado ADV fighter. This jet served with all the RAF Coningsby-based units, as well as those at RAF Leuchars. It also 'did its time' in the Falklands. It is today one of the surviving handful of aircraft still in service and is captured in this shot undertaking a low-level sortie over Wales during May 2009.

ZG778 AS140	First flew 20.05.92. Delivered to Leuchars 16.06.92, becoming 'HC'/111 Sqn during 07.92. Noted 02.93 unmarked at Leuchars. To 'A5'/56 [R] Sqn (no marks) by 07.93. To 29 Sqn 10.93 (code 'BG' allocated). Loaned to 111 Sqn before transfer to 5 Sqn in 11.98 but returned to Leuchars and used by both 43 and 111 Sqns utilising the code 'WG' by 03.04 although noted flying unmarked in 05.03. To 1435 Flt 21.11.04 by VDA An-124 becoming 'H' ('Hope'). Returned to UK 16.01.08 and taken by road to Leeming for RTP.
ZG780 AS141	Delivered 09.07.92 and first noted unmarked at Coningsby during 07.92, to 'BH' /29 Sqn during 08.92. Loaned to 11 Sqn during 11.92, returning to 29 Sqn by 12.92; loaned to the Leeming Wing 11.93. Airspare for the 1435 Flt deployment 21.10.95 and may have replaced ZE209 as 'H' ('Hope'). Noted Coningsby 05.97 and with 43 Sqn 01.99. Noted flying unmarked in 10.00 to 25 Sqn as 'WF' by 10.01 and loaned to 11 Sqn by 05.02. Received special markings with black tail with 'XXV and 1915–2005' on tail in 09.05 Altered to read 1915–2008 in 08.07. To Leeming RTP 25.06.08.
ZG793 AS142	Delivered 06.08.92. First noted unmarked with 5 Sqn during 08.92. Loaned to 11 Sqn 10.92, returning to 5 Sqn by 12.92. Coded 'CY' during 03.93, and formed part of the static line-up at Marham on 01.04.93 for the Royal Review. Loaned to the Leeming Wing 11.93. Loaned to F3OEU in 09.97 for JTIDS trials with USN at Oceana NAS. Received revised unit markings in 07.99 of a maple leaf with a yellow 5 replaced by the Roman numeral 'V'. Noted unmarked with 56 [R] Sqn 05.02 and 11 Sqn in 10.02. Coded 'DM' in 08.04 noted with hybrid 11/56 [R] Sqn marks in 05.05. To 'WM'/56 Sqn 04.06 and wfu 10.07 and flown to Leeming for RTP 07.08.

'Blacksmith 3 & 4' seen over the North Sea on 20 July 2006. Nearest is ZE257, having been recoded with the squadron from 'UB' to 'GI' in 2005. Outboard is ZG797/GF, which reflects the squadron motto *Gloria Finas*, in a special black-finned scheme and high-visibility squadron motif. This latter example was one of the final Tornado F.3s to be assigned to 1435 Flight in the Falkland Islands. Both have now been reduced to spares and their carcasses scrapped.

ZG795 AS143	Delivered to Coningsby 02.09.92, becoming 'AY'/56 [R] Sqn (no marks) later the same month. Transferred to 'CB'/5 Sqn by 05.94 remaining with the unit until being flown to the Falkland Islands for 1435 Flt in 04.00 as 'H' ('Hope'). Returned to the UK by C-17A on 02.12.01 and re-assigned to 56 [R] Sqn as 'WD'. To 111 Sqn by 10.02 but returned to 1435 Flt by C-17A on 27.11.02 until 01.02.04 upon return being assigned to 111 Sqn. With 56 [R] Sqn in 06.04 then 111 Sqn and finally 43 Sqn in 10.05 with whom it was wfu and placed into store. To Leeming by 09.06 for RTP.
ZG796 AS144	Delivered to Coningsby 15.10.92, becoming 'AV'/56 [R] Sqn during 11.92 (no marks), but with 5 Sqn as 'CE' by 10.94. To 1435 Flt in 03.98 as 'D' ('Desperation'), returning to the UK on 02.10.99. Issued to 56 [R] Sqn as 'AS' 08.00 then recoded 'WC' in 12.01. Finally with 111 Sqn before being wfu at Leeming for spares recovery in 10.05.
ZG797 AS145	Delivered to Coningsby 23.10.92. Noted unmarked with 56 [R] Sqn during 11.92, becoming 'AU'/no marks later that same month. Flown to Eielson AFB, Alaska 04.93 for Exercise Distant Frontier 93. To 29 Sqn during 10.93 still wearing 'AU' code (believed allocated 'BF'). Loaned to the Leeming Wing during 11.93. With 29 Sqn 'BF' by 08.94 before being loaned to the BAE Systems trials fleet. Re-assigned as 'GI'/43 Sqn in 11.98 before a period on loan with 11 Sqn. To 5 Sqn still in 43 marks 11.00 before recoding 'CS'. To 56 [R] Sqn and coded 'WB' in 07.01. To 11 Sqn 06.02 and back with 43 Sqn in 10.03. In 06.04 it was coded 'GF' and received 43 Sqn special marks with black tail and spine. To 1435 Flt as 'C' ('Charity') before returning to 43 Sqn by 12.06. Once again to 1435 Flt on 11.04.07 returning to the UK 16.10.09 as part of the final Tornado F.3 deployment and sent to Leeming for RTP.

ZG798 AS146	Delivered to Coningsby 19.11.92, becoming 'CS'/5 Sqn later that month. To 'CD'/5 Sqn 04.93 (no unit marks by mid-06.93). To 1435 Flt 05.97 as 'F' ('Faith') returning in 09.98. To 'AP'/56 [R] Sqn but still sporting 1435 marks. To St Athan store by 09.00 until re-issued to 25 Sqn by 09.01 still in 1435 Flt marks and coded 'AP' Assigned the code 'WA'. Loaned to 5 Sqn in 10.01 and to 56 [R] Sqn again in 07.02. Transferred to 43 Sqn by 11.02 becoming 'GQ' by 08.04. Again to 1435 Flt this time by C-17A ZZ172 on 29.03.05 as 'F' ('Faith'). Returned to the UK 08.06 for 56 [R] Sqn but back with 43 Sqn as 'GQ' by 11.06. Wfu Leuchars 05.08 and sent to Leeming 26.06.08 for RTP.
ZG799 AS147	Delivered to Coningsby 19.11.92. To 'AQ'/56 [R] Sqn by 12.92 (no marks). With 'BB'/29 Sqn 10.94 and assigned to 1435 Flt as 'D' ('Desperation') 21.09.96. Returned to UK 03.98 and with 5 Sqn by 03.99 where it was allocated the code 'CI'. To St Athan for CSP mods 10.99 it was then transferred to 43 Sqn as 'GP' but not clear whether carried. To 'VS' by 02.02 and again to 1435 Flt this time by An-124 on 22.04.03 as 'H' ('Hope'). Returned to the UK by VDA An-124 26.11.04 to St Mawgan then by road to St Athan arriving 29.11.04. To 'HJ'/111 Sqn 07.05 but wfu and flown to Leeming for RTP 17.04.08.
ZH552 ATO44 (Originally KT001)	Delivered to Coningsby 11.09.92, becoming 'AZ'/56 [R] Sqn by 10.92. Loaned to A&AEE 04.93 for JTIDS trials (returned for further work with the F3OEU by 06.93). Received 'AWC' markings in 06.94 and then revised markings in 05.96. Loaned to 11 Sqn 10.96 before becoming 'BS'/29 Sqn and then 'CH'/5 Sqn in 10.98. To 'AB'/56 [R] Sqn 02.00, 5 Sqn 02.02, 11 Sqn 10.03 and back with 56 [R] Sqn 09.04. Transferred to Leuchars for 43 Sqn 03.09 before passing onto 111 Sqn 07.09 as 'HW', with whom it is still current.

Tornado F.3 ZH553/RT in No.XI Squadron markings seen in refuelling area 6 off Newcastle on 18 June 2003, whilst operating as 'Savage 1'. Interestingly this jet was assigned the code 'DY' with No.XI Squadron but appears to have never carried this, even though it was subsequently reported as such with both 111 Squadron and 56 [R] Squadron. It is now stored at RAF Shawbury in No.56 [R] Squadron marks but still coded RT.

Qinetiq at Boscombe Down has, over the years, had a number of Tornado F.3s on strength for the test and evaluation of a number of systems. These aircraft are also often used by the Empire Test Pilots School within their course structure. Currently there are a couple of F.3s at Boscombe Down, primarily involved in Meteor missile trials. Here ZH556/HT in the markings of 111 Squadron but flown by a crew from Boscombe Down is seen low level in LFA7 on 14 February 2007.

ZH553 AT045 (Originally KT002)	First noted at Coningsby 27.01.93 (possible delivery date). By 02.93 flying unmarked with 29 Sqn, taking up the code 'BY' with the unit in 03.93. Took part in Royal Review static display at Marham on 01.04.93. Deployed for Exercise Distant Frontier 93 to Eielson AFB, Alaska during 04.93. Loaned to 11 Sqn before assigned to 56 [R] Sqn becoming 'AB' by 01.02. Loaned to 43 Sqn. Recoded 'RT' and to 11 Sqn by 05.03 before being assigned the code 'DY'. Loaned to 111 Sqn and to 56 [R] Sqn in 11.05 before passing into storage at Shawbury on 17.03.08, interestingly still coded 'RT'.
ZH554 AT046 (Originally KT003)	Delivered to Coningsby 27.01.93, transferring to Leuchars by 03.93. To 'GJ'/43 Sqn by 04.93. Participated in static display for the Royal Review at Marham 01.04.93. To 29 Sqn 11.93 (code 'BZ' allocated). To 'AP'/56 [R] Sqn by 10.99 then loaned to the F3OEU and then BAE Systems on 12.07.00. Back with F3OEU by 09.00 until 05.06 when it was re-assigned to 56 [R] Sqn with the code 'QT' allocated. In full marks by 08.06 then transferred to Leuchars and used by 43 Sqn and 111 Sqn but still in previous markings, although allocated 'HX' currently.

ZH555 AT047 (Originally KT004)	Delivered during 01.93. To 5 Sqn by 04.93 as 'CV'/special marks to mark the squadron's 80th anniversary (the 'V' of the code being a gold Roman numeral as presented on the unit's standard fin marking; also of note is that the last '5' of the serial is double normal size). These had reverted to their normal size by 08.95. Loaned to 56 [R] Sqn it once again received special markings depicting the legend '1913–2002' in 05.02 to mark the units disbandment. Transferred to 56 [R] Sqn by 09.02 and assigned the code 'PT' in 02.03. Incurred a wheels-up landing at Leuchars 04.12.03 and taken by road to St Athan 19.07.04 for repairs. Re-issued to 111 Sqn by 07.05 and then 43 Sqn in 03.06 where it was allocated the code 'GX' but probably never carried. Assigned code 'GT' in 10.07 but still marked as 'PT'/111 Sqn. Put into short term store at Leuchars before being transferred to Qinetiq as part of the Meteor missile trial in 03.09 and current.
ZH556 AT048 (Originally KT005)	Delivered to Coningsby 27.01.93. Flying unmarked with 5 Sqn 02.93. To 'AK'/56 [R] Sqn 03.93, taking part in the Royal Review static display at Marham on 01.04.93. Deployed to Eielson AFB, Alaska for Exercise Distant Frontier 93 during 04.93. Recoded 'OT' in 02.02 and assigned to 111 Sqn eventually becoming 'HT' in 06.04 but operated in hybrid marks with 56 Sqn phoenix emblem and 111 Sqn fin tip marks. To JTEG Boscombe Down 01.06 and wfu in 2009 and flown to Leeming for RTP 26.01.09.
ZH557 AT049 (Originally KT006)	Delivered to Coningsby 24.03.93. To 'AB'/56 [R] Sqn 04.93 (no marks). Operating with the A&AEE during 12.93. To 'CT'/5 Sqn by 04.94 and 'BY'/29 Sqn 01.97. To 'AF'/56 [R] Sqn then onto 111 Sqn 06.98 where it was allocated the code 'X'. To 'CT'/5 Sqn with new-style unit markings 10.00 and recoded 'NT' 11.01. With 25 Sqn 10.02, 11 Sqn 10.03 and back with 56 [R] Sqn in 05.05. Stored Leeming 25.09.06 but RTS with 25 Sqn and then 56 [R] Sqn in 06.07. After a period with 43 Sqn it was flown to Leeming 06.10.09 for RTP.
ZH558 AT050 (Originally KT007)	Delivered to Leuchars 24.03.93. To 'GF'/43 Sqn 05.93, but lost in an accident on approach to Akrotiri some 10 miles off the coast on 07.07.94.
ZH559 AT051 (Originally KT008)	Delivered to Coningsby 24.03.93, the final F.3 variant for the RAF. To 'AO'/56 [R] Sqn 04.93 (no marks) although later to be fully marked. Recoded 'AJ' by 07.95 and 'MT' in 04.02. Loaned to 43 Sqn 10.03 but back with 56 [R] Sqn by 05.05, but wearing hybrid 43/56 [R] marks. To Leeming for RTP 01.12.08.

CHAPTER 22
ATTRITION

ATTRITION IS A fact of life in any air force, in spite of all the training and preventative measures taken to avoid such incidents happening. However, the air defence world, particularly when operating twin-engine aeroplanes, suffer less than their strike/attack cousins simply because of the environment they operate in.

In over thirty years of Tornado ADV operation there have only been sixteen complete losses and two of those occurred with the Royal Saudi Air Force following a mid-air collision.

It is safe to say that of those RAF aeroplanes lost, the bulk were lost following technical malfunctions rather than aircrew error. None have been lost to hostile action.

Tragically some of these crashes have seen the loss of human life; none more so than the first to occur in June 1989 involving aircraft ZE833 and the latest, and hopefully the last, involving ZE982 on 2 July 2009, when the aircraft crashed into the hillside whilst negotiating Glen Kinglas in Argyleshire.

The RAF's first Tornado F.3 loss, involving ZE833 of No.23 Squadron, occurred during a practice intercept over the sea at relatively low level. According to the Board of Enquiry ZE833 had led the 'target pair' of aircraft for the first interception at 250ft, 400 knots on a northerly heading. Following an uneventful intercept the aircraft had climbed to 4,000ft and rolled wings level and dropped nose down. At approximately 1,000ft 67 degrees of sweep was selected and began to pitch the nose up slowly. The navigator, who had been 'watching his six', became aware of a lower than normal nose down attitude and on looking forward and checking the altimeter he shouted a warning to the pilot just as the radar altimeter low height warning, which was set at 200ft, activated.

Both crew ejected just as the tail of the aircraft struck the water and was engulfed in a fireball. The navigator survived with minor injuries but the pilot sustained multiple injuries resulting in the loss of his life.

It was four years before the RAF lost its second Tornado F.3. On 21 October 1993 during a sortie where four Tornado F.3s were

escorting a pair of Tornado GR.1s and were being pitted against an attacking force of other Tornado F.3s from another station.

Some 40 minutes into the sortie the aircraft, ZE858 from No.43 Squadron, suffered a massive fuel leak which caused a power loss to the port engine. The pilot initiated recovery to a diversion airfield and applied full reheat to climb away from low level. Unfortunately this ignited the vapour trail of fuel and caused fires in the jet pipes of both engines.

Being unable to extinguish the fires the crew ejected with the aircraft crashing into moorland near to the A66 road at Stainmore, Cumbria.

The subsequent investigation revealed that a clamp used in the connection of a feed pipe to an engine component had fractured and that this was the primary cause of the accident.

Engine fires are always a major problem to modern-day aircraft, in spite of the inbuilt safety systems. ZE809, being operated by a

Tornado F.3 ZE858 'FB' of No.25 Squadron seen at RAF Finningley in September 1989. The aircraft became the second F.3 to be lost on 21 October 1993 whilst on the strength of No.43 (F) Squadron following an in-flight fire.

The loss of ZE789 whilst with No.56 [R] Squadron on 10 March 1995 was particularly tragic with the navigator having managed to eject when the jet got into difficulties off Spurn Head only to lose his life when it is thought he was struck by the canopy as it was jettisoned. The aircraft is seen here in service with No.XI Squadron shortly after delivery.

crew from No.11 Squadron on 7 June 1994, was lost in just that way when a labyrinth seal around the High Pressure (HP) shaft had failed leading to an overheat of the shaft itself and subsequent fire.

The crew in this instance were able to eject safely after the engine warning captions had illuminated and the rear of the aircraft had become engulfed in flames. The aircraft crashed into the sea some 45 miles north-east of Scarborough.

A similar accident occurred on 17 November 1999 to ZE830 from the F3OEU based at RAF Coningsby. On this occasion the crew were conducting a night low-level navigation exercise when they heard unusual noises from their left-hand engine, followed by cockpit indications of left engine failure. Shortly afterwards, the right-hand engine bay fire caption illuminated and being at night the crew saw clear signs of fire to the rear of their aircraft.

The crew ejected and the aircraft crashed approximately 1km off the coast. Subsequent investigation established that a left engine HPC stage 1 stator vane had probably failed, and that this had led to catastrophic engine damage and a titanium fire within the engine.

On the other hand, as with the loss of ZH558 from No.43 Squadron on 8 July 1994, aircrew were not absolved from making critical errors themselves.

On this occasion the aircraft crashed into the sea on recovery to RAF Akrotiri and in spite of an exhaustive inquiry the Board could only conclude that the accident was caused by the failure of the crew to monitor the descent and, in turn, to prevent a situation where the aircraft could not be recovered prior to impact with the sea.

Unfortunately, nobody ever said that flying wasn't dangerous, however professional you are. Tornado F.3 ZE789 from No.56 Squadron at RAF Coningsby was recovering to base as a singleton on the morning of 10 March 1995 when it suffered an uncontained left-hand engine failure that was to cause severe damage to the flying controls and subsequent loss of control of the aircraft.

Both crew were able to eject before the aircraft crashed into the North Sea some 15 miles east of Spurn Head. Unfortunately the navigator was killed during the ejection sequence.

The subsequent investigation determined that the cause of the engine failure was due to thermal fatigue in the high-pressure nozzle guide vanes. Further it was thought, but not determined, that the navigator had probably been struck by the canopy as it was jettisoned.

In today's high-tech, all-weather environment, crews have to able to operate and fight in not only poor weather but also at night. The use of Night Vision Goggles (NVGs) has now become common place; that said, night is sometimes a far more dangerous place than day.

On 30 October 1995, whilst undertaking work-up for an operational detachment to the former Republic of Yugoslavia, two aircraft from No.43 Squadron collided over the North Sea some 56 nautical miles east of RAF Leuchars.

ZE733 was one of a formation of two Tornado F.3s when, during join-up at night on NVGs, they collided. As a result of the collision, control of ZE733 was lost and the crew were forced to eject. The other aircraft, ZE210, was damaged extensively in the collision but the crew managed to recover to RAF Leuchars. This jet was sent to RAF St Athan where all major work on the Tornado F.3 fleet was carried out and although initially declared 'CAT 3' and therefore repairable, the drawdown in the F.3 fleet eventually decreed that it was beyond economical repair and it was subsequently reclassified as 'CAT 5' and struck off charge.

Even in daylight the airspace can be a dangerous environment. On 10 January 1996, there was a collision during a sortie from RAF

Coningsby involving three of No.56 Squadron's aircraft, designed as part of the short course syllabus for the benefit of the pilot of ZE862, an experienced air defence pilot who had recently returned from an overseas exchange tour and was converting to the Tornado F.3.

The sortie was a 2 *v.* 1 engagement, re-introducing the pilot to the techniques required when two Tornado F.3s co-ordinate an attack on a single target. ZE166 was acting as target aircraft and crewed by OCU staff and during the engagement ZE862 collided with the target aircraft.

When the opposing aircraft had closed to a distance of 5 nautical miles, the crew of ZE166 had carried out a simulated missile attack on the left-hand aircraft (No.1 in the formation). Shortly afterwards, the crew of ZE166 saw ZE862, which was still descending, and the pilot began to manoeuvre his aircraft to attempt to carry out a simulated missile attack on it. He quickly realised that this was not going to be possible and attempted to manoeuvre away but the two aircraft collided right wing to right wing. The pilot of ZE862, which had lost approximately two-thirds of its right wing and 2 to 3ft of right taileron, initiated command ejection and due to the damage to the aircraft, both crew sustained major injuries. The pilot of ZE166, which had lost 6ft of its right wing, similarly unable to control his aircraft, also initiated command ejection. Both aircraft crashed in open country some 8 nautical miles west of RAF Coningsby.

On 15 June 1996, during the second practice intercept of a 2 *v.* 1 intercept sortie, Tornado F.3 ZE732 from No.29 Squadron had commenced a descent from 14,000ft to low level to intercept a Hawk aircraft acting as target for the sortie at 2,000ft.

The weather was not particularly good with cloud between 10,000 and 7,000ft and again from 2,000ft to almost sea level. The Tornado established a 15 degree nose down attitude passing through the layers of cloud but it was not until the Low Altitude Warning sounded at 225ft that the pilot attempted to effect recovery by which time he was too low. The aircraft impacted the sea some 30 nautical miles north-east of Flamborough Head and broke up with loss of both crew.

It is not always equipment or aircrew failure that contribute towards accidents. When ZE962 from 111 Squadron was lost shortly after take-off from RAF Leuchars when it departed normal flight, it was an accident that should never have happened.

The lead aircraft of this three-ship seen en route to Alaska in April 1992 is ZE210. The jet was involved in a mid-air collision with ZE733 and although recovered safely was struck off charge as beyond economical repair when the Tornado force began airframe reductions.

Seen landing at RAF Coningsby on 17 March 1988, shortly after delivery to No.5 Squadron. The jet, ZE732, crashed into the sea off Flamborough Head on 15 June 1998 whilst in the employ of No.29 Squadron.

The aircraft was on a transit flight from RAF Leuchars to RAF Leeming as a 'QRA' positioning flight on 14 October 2005. The jet had been unserviceable earlier in the day when it required the right flap APT to be replaced. The uncommon repair, however, had been conducted without due supervision and by someone who believed from previous experience that the flap positioning requirements were incorrect in their methodology. As a consequence, laid down procedure was deviated from and this had a direct bearing on the loss of control. Fortunately both crew were able to eject safely although both suffered some injury.

The final very tragic loss to occur involved aircraft ZE982, once a fleet leader in technology advances and part of the F3OEU trio. Its loss on 2 July 2009 was all the more tragic in that with it went the loss of both aircrew. The pilot was a young first tourist or 'dilutee' in the first two years of his tour with only 180 hours on type and his navigator a more senior member of the squadron on his fifth flying tour with 2,930 hours on type.

The incident happened as ZE982 was the leader of a pair using call-sign 'Blacksmith 1' that were negotiating a low-level route to the west of Perth. The sortie had originally planned to commence with a practice 'QRA' intercept profile controlled by an E-3 Sentry AWACS aircraft followed by a low-level navigation exercise. The E-3, however, advised the crews that it would be late on task, so the navigation exercise was re-planned.

The pair of Tornados had descended into the low-level around Strathallen before turning south down Loch Lomond then west at Tarbet to follow the A83 road via the viewpoint at Rest and Be Thankful and into Glen Kinglas where it struck the north slope at 1198ft above mean sea level.

The Board of Inquiry concluded that the cause of the accident was due to insufficient turning room being available within the valley to complete the turn as executed, with the inference that lack of pilot experience was a contributory factor to the accident happening, which only goes to prove the necessity of learning and maintaining those flying skills. Flying is dangerous and only good practice and experience can reduce the risk of such accidents happening.

Considered at one point the fleet leader in upgrades, ZE982, while on the strength of No.43 (F) Squadron, crashed into the hillside of Glen Kinglas in Argyleshire on 2 July 2009. This was the last of twelve Tornado F.3s to be lost and again in tragic circumstances that led to the loss of both crew. The report highlighted the lack of experience on the part of the pilot, particularly in the low level, and this has caused concerns across the board, including those in NATO that have voiced their concerns, over the UK's reduction in flying hours to a figure significantly below those of the NATO minimum. In this shot the jet is seen en route from Oceana NAS, Virginia, where it had been conducting JTIDS trials with the F3OEU.

Visit our website and discover thousands of other History Press books.
www.thehistorypress.co.uk